BECOMING A LIBRARY TEACHER

W9-AMP-053

...TINE **K. OKA**

...eries

NEAL-SCHUMAN PUBLISHERS, INC.

NEW YORK   LONDON

The New Library Series

No. 1 – *Finding Common Ground: Creating the Library of the Future without Diminishing the Library of the Past*. Edited by Cheryl LaGuardia and Barbara A. Mitchell.

No. 2 – *Recreating the Academic Library: Breaking Virtual Ground*. Edited by Cheryl LaGuardia.

No. 3 – *Becoming A Library Teacher: Power Strategies for Delivering Instruction*. By Cheryl LaGuardia and Christine K. Oka

Published by Neal-Schuman Publishers, Inc.
100 Varick Street
New York, NY 10013

Copyright © 2000 by Cheryl LaGuardia

Printed and bound in the United States of America.

ISBN 1–55570–378–X

DEDICATION

We dedicate this book to our families, who have taught us so much.

CONTENTS

FIGURES

PREFACE

"Truth persuades by teaching, but does not teach by persuading."

Tertullian, *Adversus Valentinianos*

In 1996, in a book entitled, *Teaching the New Library*, the chapter called, "Finding, Creating, Becoming Library Teachers" briefly discussed how to identify potential teachers, and then touched on the performance aspects of library teaching, as well as how to put classes together and teach them.

In the years since *Teaching the New Library* was published, library colleagues said they wished that chapter had gone into much greater detail about how to become a library teacher because it just whetted their appetites for more. The reply was always "Well, that would be a whole 'nother book." And so it is.

When we were learning how to become library teachers (and it wasn't all that long ago), there was no library instruction manual out there. When we went to library school, there were no formal library instruction courses offered. We had to make up our library teaching as we went along. Teaching can be an isolating experience, since it's often you up there in front of the class by yourself. It was in the days when we thought we were in it all by ourselves—that we were alone in the wilderness of learning how to teach—that we could most have used some help, or at least some communication with the rest of the world. Going through what was, at times, an unnecessarily painful learning process, we vowed that someday we'd write a book that could save others from suffering needlessly as we did.

We want to share with you as many as possible of the library instruction tricks of the trade we've collected. Before we do that, however, we should acknowledge that these ARE tricks of the trade: they are not educational theories or hypothetical methodologies, but rather are the building block techniques we think new teachers will find useful for entering the classroom.

The nitty-gritty aspects of library instruction are not covered very much in the library literature, or at least, not covered in the way we're addressing them here. If you do a few searches in Library Literature and ERIC, you'll find more articles and essays on cognitive learning theory and conceptual frameworks than you can shake a stick at, and they're done by learned people who know these theories well and generally articulate them beautifully.

Our book turns theory into practice. We will help you get past any stage fright or fear of presenting. We plan to teach you how to actually apply your skills and knowledge to the learning needs of your students. But we warn you: we are renegades in the field of library instruction—we don't "do it by the book," so to speak—and you may need to keep this tome at your desk covered in a brown paper wrapper.

We strongly believe that if you approach library instruction as just another job of work, becoming a library teacher will be much easier, and less intimidating than if you invest teaching with an arcane "mystique." Teaching is not a gift. It's not something some people can do and others can't. Neither is it a fixed set of concepts and methodologies you will learn just by studying and researching the topic.

Teaching is something you ultimately learn (or at least learn how to do well) by . . . doing it. There ARE rules you can follow to learn how to do it. And by all means, please do study and research the topic in both the library and educational literature: having a good grounding in educational theory can give you an excellent context for learning how to teach. We'd all love to study the literature and take weeks to put together a practice class. Real life often doesn't feature the luxury of time. Our focus is the here and now of library teaching. We assume your job of becoming a library teacher might begin as soon as tomorrow.

We've divided this book into two distinct, yet interwoven parts. Part 1, Library Instruction as Performance, is devoted to the presentation (well, showmanship) techniques that are the basis for good instruction: how to get up in front of a group of people, talk to them, and sit back down—without going to pieces. You can do this. Trust us, and read on.

In Part 2, Composing Classes, we discuss approaches to library classes themselves: how to develop class outlines and syllabi and ways of teaching library concepts to those who do not necessarily plan on becoming librarians—or even full-time researchers—themselves. We touch on learning styles (from a highly subjective standpoint), describe information gathering, discuss how sensitivity to student diversity can—and should—be incorporated into classes, and suggest ways the various kinds of library classes and presentations can be put together. We can't tell you exactly what each class will look like, because good library class content responds to local users' needs. But we can, and do, offer practical guidelines for how to approach a class and put it together.

As the title indicates, this book is about the process of becoming a library teacher. We're not trying here to cover the full gamut of library teaching methodology, since many of those issues (assessing instructional needs, developing specific teaching methods, related readings, etc.) are covered in the companion volume to this work, *Teaching the New Library* (LaGuardia, et al. 1996. Neal-Schuman). *Becoming a Library Teacher* provides groundwork for *Teaching the New Library*.

This book provides the building block techniques you'll need before you actually start teaching. You may use *Becoming a Library Teacher* and *Teaching the New Library* together or alone. Each offers librarians in the making, as well as practicing front-line librarians, the "real life" means of getting into the library classroom and staying there successfully.

Here's the book we wish we'd had in our hot little hands when we were starting out to become library teachers. It's based entirely on our personal experiences, so the techniques described have all been put to the test firsthand (aka, we're not trying to sell you a theoretical pig in a poke: this stuff has worked for us and for colleagues). If you feel isolated out there, we hope that by reading this book you will know you're not alone. We, and many others committed to library instruction, are right there with you.

Cheryl LaGuardia
Christine K. Oka

ACKNOWLEDGMENTS

We'd like to thank our library colleagues—those with whom we've taught and worked over the years, as well as those whom we've seen teach and speak—for helping us become library teachers. Our particular thanks to the core group of colleagues with whom we learned to teach at the University of California at Santa Barbara library: Adan Griego (El Jefé), Michael Hopper, Chuck Huber, and Lisa Melendez. We learned from all of you, and are grateful.

Special thanks to Michele LaGuardia for reading the first draft of this manuscript and giving us the benefit of her 17 years' teaching experience with invaluable additions and edits.

Cheryl adds her heartfelt thanks to Michele for giving her the nerve to enter the classroom that first time. If you really want to learn how to teach, pray for a sister who will give you an hour lecture about role-playing and how to "scare 'em." You find the nerve, all right.

Part One

LIBRARY INSTRUCTION AS PERFORMANCE

Chapter 1

NERVOUS, ANYONE? PERFORMANCE ANXIETY

On the stage he was natural, simple, affecting;
'Twas only that when he was off he was acting.
Oliver Goldsmith, *Retaliation*

Many of us became librarians precisely because we wanted to avoid getting up in front of groups. Unfortunately for those of us who thought we'd figured out the system and beaten it, the reality in today's library is that you're probably going to be presenting daily, or at least weekly, to some group or other. It may be staff training, or a tour, or a computer demonstration, but it will be instructional in nature and it will typically be for more than one or two people at a time. Surprise! Bummer!

It's time for a show of hands. Anybody out there who is not in the least intimidated at the prospect of getting up and speaking in front of a group of people? Hmmm. A few hands are in the air, but most of you suddenly seem awfully quiet and . . . anxious? Well, for those of you who raised your hands in the affirmative to our question, just skip all of Part One and move right on into the rest of the book. Lucky you—have a nice day.

For the rest of the 99.27% of us folks, let's face the bogeyman and talk about fear of public speaking. We came across an article some years ago in which it was stated that most people fear public speaking more than either death or financial ruin—no contest.[1] In surveys and reports we've read on phobias, fear of public speaking is always among the first two or three most frequently listed fears, and often ranks as number one. [2,3]

Why is this? We don't know the specific reasons, except that potential humiliation and public censure probably figure largely into it. It's one thing to make a fool of yourself quietly in life, in one-on-one situations, or to expose your ignorance to one or two people at a time. But to get up and say things in a public forum for everyone present to see, hear, and possibly ridicule seems like, well, not a great idea, unless you are a fairly masochistic sort of person (no, please, put your hands down, that was not a question for which we were seeking an answer from among our readers. We don't want to know).

We don't pretend to any psychological expertise in this area: all we have to work with is our personal experience, being basically shy, introverted people who were petrified, at one time, at the thought of getting up and speaking in front of groups and who now, through an ironic twist of fate, make our livings by doing just that.

Suffice it to say that we were dragged, if not kicking and screaming, at least unwillingly, into the instructional fray. Neither of us had any formal education for teaching, neither of us had any training or coaching in public speaking. Both of us were initially terrified of teaching. And almost overnight we were faced with the prospect of having teaching become our main responsibility.

We hope this is not the situation you are facing, but would not be surprised if it were. Because the reality we've witnessed in libraries is that the nature of the work is changing at a very elemental level, and the main change that's taking place is the incorporation of teaching responsibilities of one kind or another into practically every real library job. Whether this is formal end user instruction in a classroom setting, or remote instruction via building and maintaining Websites, or in-house staff training (either group-based or individual), most librarians are becoming teachers on the job.

The reason we said we hoped this was not the situation you are facing is because, obviously, in the best of circumstances, it is preferable to prepare in advance for this kind of work rather than suddenly to be thrust into it with little or no warning. If you are a library school student reading this, you may be somewhat discomfited to hear that your professional life can change so dramatically so unexpectedly. Welcome to the real world—the sooner you get used to working within a climate of constant change and revision the sooner you can count yourselves true librarians (and the more likely you will find and keep work within the profession). For the rest of our readers: if you've worked in a library for longer than six months you are probably already aware of both points we've made in the last few paragraphs: that your job requirements can change remarkably fast and that some kind of instructional duties will probably fall to your lot.

If this fact makes you feel panicky, welcome to the club. We have been there, believe us: we know what it's like to feel like you're going to pass out (or suddenly go mentally blank, or make mistakes, or lose your voice, or have the computer go down, or spontaneously combust . . . who ever said these were rational fears? The whole point is the irrationality of the public speaking phobia . . .). The main reason we're writing this book is to help others avoid the trauma that can come from trying to learn how to teach. So whether you are a librarian-in-progress or a librarian de facto, we urge you to address your teaching terrors as soon as possible. And we intend to help you face them down.

REFERENCES

1. Conlin, Elizabeth. 1990. "It's Showtime." *Inc.* 7 (July): 25.
2. Schrof, Joannie. 1999. "Why Everyone Gets Stage Fright." *U.S. News & World Report*, 126 (June 21): 57.
3. Wallechinsky, David, Irving Wallace, and Amy Wallace. 1977. "The Fourteen Worst Human Fears." *The Book of Lists*. New York: William Morrow and Company.

Chapter 2

TAMING TEACHING TERROR

. . . Possess them not with fear; take from them now
The sense of reckoning, if the opposed numbers
Pluck their hearts from them.

Shakespeare, *Henry V*

The original title of this chapter was, "Presentation Techniques" (which may have appealed to the less luridly-inclined among our readers), but we decided instead to call it as we saw—and felt—it and so renamed it as you see above.

The phrase "Presentation Techniques" conjures up for us images of quietly composed professional people in dark blue suits with white blouses or shirts and red ties standing in front of a long tableful of other similarly attired professionals. The presenters (standing) are handing out tidy portfolios of information to their colleagues, and are obviously cool, calm, collected, and about to make the presentation of their dreams.

Cut to reality, in the grim, amorphous shape of Teaching Terror. The phrase brings out the primal instincts most of us share about public speaking: the mouth goes dry and the sweat glands open just saying it. When we were first teaching, every upcoming class was torture, both real and imagined. The prospect of having to teach haunted us for days in advance, we worried, dreaded, anguished, wildly prepared, and then went through the harrowing experience, somehow getting it over—only to start the process again when next we were scheduled to teach.

With time and experience some of the typical pre-presentation panic symptoms lessened. But they never go away completely—we are both still "wired" just before a class. Our perceptions are heightened, our senses are all just a little bit on edge, and we think we know, just a little, of what a prizefighter experiences when he climbs into the ring.

That wired feeling of climbing into the ring is very different, however, from the teaching terror we used to feel. The wired feeling is more anticipation and exhilaration—anticipating the rush that comes from a good class—than any performance anxiety. And that, of course, is what we're talking about here: performance anxiety.

Every good performer has some performance anxiety, whether it is the bracing exhilaration noted above or knee-knocking, teeth-rattling fear. In fact, if you get to the point where you are no longer experiencing any performance anxiety, you might want to ask a colleague or two to observe and give you some feedback about your teaching, because renewal may be in order. A total lack of performance anxiety can be a sign of teaching overload or burnout.

As with any kind of performance, the first task is to tame the terror—turning it into a manageable anxiety, if you will. So here are the tricks of the trade—the physical, mental, and organizational preparation techniques—we use to tame our teaching and presentation terrors.

Chapter 3

PREPARING YOURSELF PHYSICALLY

The human body is an instrument for the production of art in the life of the human soul.
Alfred North Whitehead, *Adventures of Ideas*

The physical preparation for a presentation involves a lot of everyday, common sense practices that really prepare you well for any life situation. But as we've also observed, there is nothing as uncommon as common sense, witnessed by the fact that we're both still guilty, at times, of arriving at the last minute for a class ("it was unavoidable!" hah!) or wearing high heels for an ALA panel presentation lasting three hours.

If you are in reasonable physical condition, that is: well rested, well fed, alert, but not so hyper from caffeine your colleagues have to pull you down off the ceiling (think of Goldilocks as the model for how you want to feel going into a class . . . not too hot, not too cold . . . juuussst right), you'll enhance your chances of teaching well. And conversely, if you don't get enough sleep the night before, if you drink four cups of coffee on an empty stomach that morning and then run to an over-heated classroom, not only will it be a miracle if your class goes well, but you may keel over in the front of the classroom.

Keeling over is not the end of the world, by the way. If you attain peak attitude, you can teach on through anything, like the colleague who literally lost her under-wear—the elastic failed—while at the chalkboard. She stepped out of 'em, tossed them on her desk, and went right on teaching. The class applauded. True story, we swear it. Now that's instructional elan. Having expressed our admiration, we don't recommend this as a practice—so try not to wear clothing that's going to fall off mid-class.

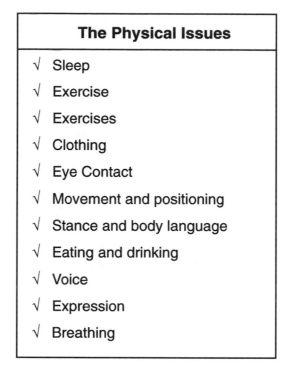

The Physical Issues

- √ Sleep
- √ Exercise
- √ Exercises
- √ Clothing
- √ Eye Contact
- √ Movement and positioning
- √ Stance and body language
- √ Eating and drinking
- √ Voice
- √ Expression
- √ Breathing

You can depend upon it that if you teach with any regularity, sometime, somewhere, you will not feel real well during a class. We have tips on how to deal with the unusual and out-of-the-ordinary situations based on personal and shared experiences, but for now let's concentrate on what's good practice for the norm rather than what to do in emergencies.

SLEEP

We're starting with what seems like an easy, no-brainer; something you've probably had drilled into you by your Mom since before you can remember: you need to get enough sleep if you want to teach well. Even as we say this, however, we have to confess that, for years, we tried to function on four to six hours of sleep a night. Were we able to? Well, we could, as long as your definition of "function" is very elastic. How long can you go on with sleep deprivation? They're trying to find out using rats, reducing the amounts drastically on the poor beggars. Most of these rats end up gonzo. Not wanting to end up gonzo, we're sleeping more these days.

Under typical circumstances, you will know when you have a class or presentation coming up. Get at least eight hours of sleep the night before any presentation, and it's even better if you can get ten, especially if it's a big (important, new, potentially challenging) presentation.

If you don't believe how much of a difference being well-rested makes to your teaching, by all means, try going on with less sleep. See how well you focus, how much energy you have throughout the class, what the dynamic with the students becomes. See if you feel like a limp rag after two classes in one day. Anybody under 30 reading this: you can get away with it for awhile, but it takes its toll. Anybody over 30 (like us) reading this: see what burning the candle at both ends got you?

If you're caught off guard with a spontaneous, unexpected presentation one day and you haven't gotten the recommended eight to ten hours sleep, take ten or twenty minutes before the class to get quiet somewhere (go deep into the stacks if you must), put your feet up, and close your eyes. Even if you can't sleep easily under such circumstances, the brief rest will help prepare you for the presentation adrenaline rush and the energy it takes to go "on."

EXERCISE

Some of you may find this item on the list surprising (others who know us may find it well-nigh astounding), but the plain truth is, if you're in decent shape you're going to do better in the classroom. Neither of us engages in heavy exercise, but we do quite a bit of walking, to keep our stamina up. When we find ourselves puffing from class to class, we walk a little more. During the deep New England winters we resort to mall walking if we can't work in anything else. We even lift small weights for upper body strength (this helps your posture and stamina, and let's face it—ya can't pound those computer keys with flabby fingers). Exercise in whatever way suits your lifestyle and abilities, but exercise somehow.

In addition to stamina and energy, exercise fits you for teaching in two other ways: breath control (much more about this later) and, for want of a better term, agility in front of the class. We move around our classrooms, even if we're doing computer demonstrations.

We attended a performance workshop once that was very good overall, with one notable exception: The instructor was trained as an actor, and insisted that workshop participants stand stock still when speaking, feet firmly rooted to the ground, hands at their sides. This is not the kind of agility we recommend. It is more natural, and a good thing, to move around the classroom. We'll talk more about this under "Movement and Positioning", but for now be advised that you usually need to be able to move around confidently, easily, and effectively to do a good class.

And in the interests of diversity, this applies to the specially-abled, as well. Movement comes in a variety of forms: legs, arms, heads, eyes, by wheelchair and walker, and interpreter and signer, all signifying a mobile and lively intellect. You need to make use of a combination of these to do a good class.

EXERCISES

So much for the idea of exercise, now what about exercises? Not sit-ups or jumping jacks, but exercises for limbering up before a presentation. And before you dismiss these as inconsequential or stupid, let us point out that we still do some, or all, of these before every class and every presentation we give because, in addition to making us more flexible and agile, they calm us down and give us something to concentrate on other than any performance anxiety we might be beginning to experience.

- Head rolls: do slow 180-degree rolls from one side to another (not full 360-degree rolls).
- Shaking hands: not from fear, but from vigorously shaking your hands out in front of you from the wrist. Clenching and unclenching your hands is another good variation on this.
- Deep grimaces: you may find yourself doing these quite naturally if you're truly averse to teaching. The point is to loosen your jaw, which tends to tighten up before public speaking. If you find yourself frowning so broadly and deeply that the cords in your neck stand out . . . you're doing these correctly.
- Face clenches: close your eyes and mouth and try to scrunch up your face as tightly as you can, then release it.
- Tongue sticking out: need we say more? Make your tongue and lips as loose and mobile as you can.
- Arm, leg, and finger stretches: reach up, reach out, reach down, extend your arms, legs, hands, and fingers until they feel looser.
- Shoulder shrugs: this one is a very handy exercise, both for loosening up the major upper body muscles that tend to get tight (and therefore make you feel like you can't breathe and like you're going to pass out) as well as for generating saliva. No kidding, it's worked for us: if you roll your shoulders forward repeatedly you'll probably find saliva forming in your mouth. Not the most delicately appealing image in the world, but a *deus ex machina* if you tend to get dry mouth before a class the way we do. As an added bonus, this one can be subtle enough that if you become expert at it, you can do it during a presentation surreptitiously and you'll never have dry mouth problems again.

Oh, yes, one thing more. The rest of these exercises are meant to be done in private, not up in the front of the classroom as the students are filing in (although we've often toyed with the idea of doing them then). There's always the ladies' or men's room available: use them if need be.

CLOTHING

There is no recommended uniform for teaching, no matter what others may try to tell you. Why do we even say this? Because we've come across some real lay-down-the-law strictures in articles and workshops on the topic of dress. Some folks try to tell you never to dress casually, others tell you not to dress too formally, still others tell you not to wear any jewelry, or running shoes, or bright colors, or dark colors, or tiaras . . . well, okay, so we stuck the tiaras in to see if you were paying attention. But for the rest, we've seen them all ruled out at one time or other.

The main two recommendations we have for teaching / presentation clothing are: 1. Wear something that makes you comfortable and confident, and 2. Layer. Our reasoning is as follows:

Presumably, something that makes you comfortable and confident is going to be something appropriate to the occasion at hand. There are circumstances under which a suit or dress (or at least slacks / skirt and a jacket) may be most appropriate. If you tend to look like an overstuffed sausage in a suit, however, like one of us does, stay away from them. Seldom do you feel comfortable and confident when dressed like a sausage. There are other options in this category that cover all body types (ouch for the pun, but we mean it anyway). If floaty and drapy suits you, then wear floaty and drapy (but do be aware that if your presentation involves much movement or working with equipment, floaty and drapy has its pitfalls. Just plan for them—make your clothing decision a conscious one, rather than a setup for "Oops! My entire right side is caught in the flip chart." Not a pretty sight).

There are other occasions when jeans and a tee shirt may work, too (GASP! We can hear the sudden communal intake of breath out there. "How unprofessional," some of you may be saying). But think about it: for some in-house workshops involving role playing, etc., casual clothing is called for. And even for some classes, more casual attire is appropriate: it all depends upon the circumstances of the class and the setting. If you do your advance homework well (described more fully in the Organizational Preparation section) you may find that a casual approach is called for and more effective for connecting with your audience. So there are no absolutes about clothing, no matter what folks may try to tell you.

Having said that, we test our own proof with the assertion that whenever possible, you should wear layers of clothing, whatever style you choose. This is for the simple reason that you seldom, if ever, can control the temperature of the classroom in which you are teaching. Even if you think you have temperature control, it can be circumvented: an overfull classroom full of computers heats up remarkably quickly, and if you tend to perspire heavily, as we do, you'll be drenched and smell like a sheep by the end of a class taught in heavy wool.

On the other hand, if you are cold most of the time, it's to be hoped you've learned by now to carry a sweater with you to the classroom. If you haven't, plan on it for the future, because if you turn the heat up in the classroom sufficiently to keep yourself warm, you will probably put the entire audience to sleep—no matter how exciting your presentation style—in the fugginess that results (a colleague in charge of room climate control managed to do this once at a national conference: drove some of an audience of over 200 out, vigorously fanning themselves, and put the rest of us into a stupor). We don't know all the ins and outs of learning theory, but we're fairly certain that putting students into a stupor is not recommended practice for making them educationally receptive. And let's face it: the typical library class is full of material that can, by its very nature, lull an audience into numbness (no, we're not saying it has to be thus, only that it easily can go that way).

And if you can't turn up the heat and you've left your sweater in your office, hope fervently that you look really, really good in blue, 'cause that's what you're gonna turn. In large lecture halls (and in computerized classrooms), it's preferable to keep the temperature low rather than high, to avoid the stupefaction quotient and to preserve the equipment. So plan accordingly.

About jewelry: we don't have strong feelings or recommendations about it. At one institution where we both taught, a group of library instructors used the talisman of a "presentation neck chain" in classes (we offered it to gentlemen and ladies alike, so no sexist intent there, honestly). It was considered good luck among us, and saw us through some sticky early attempts. It also fostered a sense of camaraderie among instructors, as we passed the chains around in a spirit of sharing. If you listen to some folks, they'll tell you never to wear anything that can get caught on a desk or a monitor screen or whatever. Use your judgment, for Pete's sake. We don't like to say "Never."

All common sense stuff, right? Do you pay attention to this all the time now? We still find ourselves wearing heavy pullover sweaters sometimes on class days, and pay for it with high dry-cleaning bills. And we often wear heavy jewelry or huge earrings or rings to classes that we end up removing so we can use a phone or move the mouse well. So long as you can maneuver through whatever challenges your clothing and accessories create, it's not a big issue—but do dress according to what the occasion, and audience, demand. It's one less thing to worry about during the presentation or class.

EYE CONTACT

This was so difficult for us at first: we never knew who to look at during our early classes. If we made eye contact with somebody in the front row and they actually met our gaze in turn, it seemed like we stared at them throughout the whole class, eventually, of course, making them extremely uncomfortable. Remember classes where the teacher was always balefully glaring at you (or so it seemed)?

On the other hand, if we tried making eye contact with students all over the room (this was a classroom with 30 computer workstations in it), we invariably found some student either nodding off or looking disgustedly back at us, which was, admittedly, discouraging to a new teacher, even if well-deserved (Note well: everybody has to learn how to teach and we freely concede that we taught some real snoozers early on. But sometimes students come to a class determined to snooze or be disgusted, and we're going to discuss this in detail in the "Confidence" section of Chapter Four).

So we struggled with this problem for years, until an expert trainer taught us the real trick: let your gaze move over the entire class, looking NO ONE in the eye. Instead, direct your gaze at the point on their foreheads between their eyebrows. Start with one side of the room and move your gaze over the whole class, one at a time, or picking out individuals in various rows at various times: but don't look anybody in the eye. Look at those foreheads.

Okay, okay, we can hear the outraged shrieks of seasoned teachers, and we'd be shrieking ourselves if we'd read this far and no farther. So read farther.

The forehead gazing technique is what we call a "start up trick," to be used just to get you comfortable in the classroom. As you gain your instructional bearings, you will be able, and you will absolutely WANT to look your students in the eye. This is one of the ways you'll get feedback from them: if you look at them and see utter confusion, chances are you need to go over at least that last point again. And if you look at the students' eyes and they're all closed, you need to pep up your presentation style: the eyes are the windows to the soul (and sleep centers).

So, for the classroom, use the forehead gazing trick only as long as you have to, and then wean yourself away from it. However, if you find yourself making a one-time presentation to a large crowd at ALA or wherever, by all means drag it out again and employ it—it works like a charm, makes you look like a terrific speaker who is meaningfully connected to your audience. And, in fact, by using this technique to be able to get up there and make the speech, you are.

MOVEMENT AND POSITIONING

Maybe the best way we can initiate this discussion is by using two extreme examples of unusual professors we had in undergraduate school, whom we'll designate here with the aliases "The Statue" and "The Acrobat." The Statue stood immobile in the front of the classroom behind a table with a podium on it. His hands clutched the podium, and he read to us directly from the text (which he had authored) for 50 minutes. He never looked up at us, never even acknowledged by word or glance our presence in the room. He stood there and read at us for 15 weeks, and the smart money among the betting folk in the class was on the firm assumption that his shoes were nailed to the floor behind that podium. (This wagering took place early in the term when some of us managed to stay awake long enough to place the bets. Later in the term, as the novelty wore off, gambling was unilaterally replaced by utter somnolence.)

The Acrobat, on the other hand, ranged over the entire front end of the classroom, performing what genuinely looked like calisthenics. He began his workout in a low key fashion, standing before us with his hands on his hips, gazing out over our heads (obviously, no one had told him about the forehead gaze). Then he would begin to do deep knee bends, slowly at first, then with increasing frequency and vigor. From the deep knee bends he would move on to side twists, first to one side, then to the other, first with hands on hips, then with arms outstretched. After that, he would raise his hands high over his head and then swing down to touch his toes. All of this while lecturing to us continuously. True, it was a little difficult to hear him when he did the toe touches, but otherwise he was perfectly audible throughout. The class would watch with increasing fascination as he went through this routine, which varied a bit, but which lasted the entire lecture. And try as we might, we could never remember much of what he said, because, of course, our attention was wholly fixed on the bizarre and increasingly exaggerated movements he was making.

Point taken? Neither extreme is going to make a good teacher out of you. Total immobility puts an audience to sleep unless you are a really, really good speaker and your subject is totally riveting. Wild antics, on the other hand, can detract from your message: they can unbalance the focus of your audience's attention to your physical presence rather than on the information you're trying to convey. And as much as we're focusing in this book on you and your becoming good library teachers, in the classroom it's not about you, it's about the class.

This should be comforting to those of you uncomfortable with being the focus of attention. Remember that in teaching, Marshall McLuhan notwithstanding, it's ultimately the message that's important, not the medium through which it's communicated.

Now about positioning. What do you do with yourself when you're in front of the class? Do you stand up? Sit down? Fight, fight, fight! Where and how to stand can be a real hurdle for many. It's a problem most actors have to confront in their very first roles, but library instructors often enter the classroom with no notion that it's an issue. That is, until they find themselves front and center with no idea of where to go from there.

If you are doing a computer demonstration the dilemma may be solved for you de facto, because the position of the computer dictates where you are going to be in the classroom, and whether you're going to be standing or sitting. This also solves the hands' dilemma ("What ARE those gawky things at the ends of my arms? And what do I do with them?"). In a computer demonstration your hands are not just hanging at your sides like forgotten, vestigial appendages: they're doing the brunt of the work for you on the keyboard. Oh happy, happy computer classes!

But what do you do in non-computerized situations? Well, if you're like some of our colleagues, you may have a tendency to back away from the class, revealing your innermost thoughts about teaching in the clearest possible way. Several colleagues leave classes with a straight line of chalk across their butts, having backed up all the way to the chalkboard (we swear we once saw a colleague climb halfway up the wall before they were pried off it). We taught in a classroom that had a post in the front of the room, and several colleagues taught much like chanteuses from those 1930's Busby Berkeley Depression-era musicals—they'd end up wound around the post as if it were a street lamp on the corner.

There is no one, right way to position yourself in a classroom: it almost always depends upon the configuration of the room, and, let's face it, library classrooms can be notoriously idiosyncratic in their layouts. The rule of thumb is: if a computer's involved and you have to station yourself at it, by all means you must, but don't stay rooted to the floor behind it. Come out from behind the computer from time to time: cross to the screen or wall on which you're projecting the computer image when there's a particularly important point and underscore it with your hand (or a laser pointer, about which more to follow). Approach the students from time to time; if you can get a dialogue going at any point, walk towards the questioner or speaker, give them your undivided attention. Moving to a few different positions around the classroom will help keep you and the students energized—just don't spend the entire class walking around the room in circles or leaping from point to point.

STANCE AND BODY LANGUAGE

If you are standing during the class, however, there is *one* right way to do it, and that's with the best possible posture. Stand up as tall as you can, firmly on your feet. Is this just our harking back again to Mom's advice? Kind of—it was good advice, especially for the purposes of teaching, because having good posture will ultimately give you more vigor and keep you from tiring easily during the class. It will also enhance good breathing techniques, making it easier for you to get fresh air in and to expel the old. And just between us, it gives you a more commanding air: if you're feeling at all trepidatious, then stand up even straighter—it can make you actually feel more confident.

About what to do with your hands if there's no computer busy work involved. You can always develop a signature gesture. Think of President Clinton's pointed finger, used for emphasis in denying . . . ah, well . . . , then there's the measured hand chop characteristic of many public speakers to make their points. But we suggest you make use of a prop, at least when you're starting out. We use a laser pointer in our classes, whether we're projecting something on the wall or not. Just having the pointer in our hands gives us something to clutch, or, looked at more aesthetically, it gives our hands something to hold in a perfectly natural, normal position. We can extend it for emphasis, and it can even be used to point at something on the wall. Just be aware that it's easy for excessive hand gestures to move you into the Acrobat's realm, and if you find yourself yearning to squat in front of the class (WHERE did those deep knee bends come from?!?) our advice is, don't. This leads us into the broader area of body language.

Body language is different from movement and positioning and stance in our minds because it's really about attitude: your attitude towards others and how you convey it. We raise the subject here because the chances are, if you are ever observed for your teaching, your body language is an area about which you will get lots of feedback. Did you face the class or keep your back to them for the most part? Did you stand or sit with your arms crossed across your chest in a protective, closed-off attitude or did you stand with arms akimbo in a more open posture? Did you approach the class during your teaching, or did you distance yourself from them? Did you approach students when they asked questions? Have you mastered eye contact or are you at least using the forehead gaze effectively? Did you sit like a bump on a log at the computer from start to finish, or did you rove around the classroom working with students (for hands-on computer classes)? Did you clutch the podium or try to hide behind a pillar or a post throughout?

We've purposely phrased these questions to get you thinking about your body language. Our purpose is to make you self-aware of your presence "on stage" in the class—it is not, however, to make you self-conscious about it. If dealing with the issue of body language and the non-verbal messages you're sending is not comfortable for you initially, don't be concerned. It's something what will come naturally with experience and the ability to distance yourself from the present in your mind's eye while teaching.

But we urge you to at least consider, in every class, the kinds of messages you may intentionally or unintentionally be sending to students with your attitudes and behaviors. It's like working at the reference desk: are you being receptive and welcoming? Or do you have your head tucked down, staring at the desktop or reading? Are you closing off your space or keeping it open to questions? You have the power to send very strong non-verbal messages up in front of a class.

EATING AND DRINKING

It may seem like we're intruding into very personal areas here, but believe us, we're not. What, and how much, you eat and drink before a class or presentation are major considerations that can have enormous impact on your performance. We've tried various strategies over the years, thinking we'd find a magic formula for how much and what to consume. Much of what we've tried is based on the supposedly sage advice of others: eat very lightly, drink no caffeine, drink a full glass of water just before you go on. And once again it seems to fall out best for us to use our own judgment: sometimes we eat a light meal before a class, other times we have a normal meal. We always do eat something however, and we try to have a combination of both carbohydrates and protein, for energy and staying power, because too often in the past we skipped a meal before going on and discovered our energy flagging halfway through (at best) or a feeling of lightheadedness and weakness overcoming us (at worst). The days of skipping meals and being able to keep a train of thought going are long past for both of us, and we advise you to avoid the practice entirely.

About beverages: this depends much more on personal preference and habits. We often bring a capped bottle of water to classes and presentations just to wet our whistles: 50 minutes' worth of talking can thoroughly dry out your throat. We drink enough water before a class to keep from becoming dehydrated, but not so much as to experience discomfort during a protracted session when we can't leave the room easily. Caffeine is a real controversial issue for many teachers: a number of performers say no caffeine is the way to go. We've tried going without caffeine, and it doesn't work for us: we become slugs. So in a fairly middle of the road approach, we usually try to ingest our normal amounts of caffeine, figuring to go under that level will set in motion withdrawal symptoms we don't need on a performance day, while to go over can make you so jumpy you'll need to be peeled off the ceiling (we've had to do this for several team teaching colleagues, and it's not pretty). We gauge the success of this approach by our motor functions in the class: too little and we barely speak, too much and we're motor mouths.

We strongly advise against any alcohol before a class—not so much for temperance reasons but because of the ultimately depressant effects. It's also not liable to build confidence in students if you're wandering around the classroom smelling like a brewery. And the real reason we bring the issue of alcohol up is because we know how sorely tempted some new teachers may be to "fortify" their resolve with a good stiff one just before having to get up in front. Don't do it—use the other tricks we're suggesting here instead—they're not harmful and will see you through without incalculable repercussions.

> *If you find yourself drinking **during** classes, or contemplating it seriously, it's possible you need to rethink becoming a library teacher. . . .*

VOICE

Your voice can be the single most powerful instrument you have for teaching, if you use it well. By powerful, we really mean versatile and effective, because you don't have to have either Pavarotti's projection capacity or a drill sergeant's shouting ability to have a voice that's a powerful instrument. In fact, a soft voice, so long as it can at least be heard throughout the room, can be a very good teaching tool, because it forces the class to pay attention, focus, and really listen to you. Remember, especially in regard to your voice, that as a teacher, you are a performer.

Think of the worst speakers you have ever heard, or even of caricatures of bad speakers. Their voices are very memorable, aren't they? Monotonic, unvarying, droning. Poor or inexperienced speakers do not vary the tones of their voices, they don't alter the rhythm during presentations, they never change pitch. They could be reading the phone book or a declaration of war and both would sound the same coming out of their mouths (and both would make nearly the same impact on their audiences).

Good speakers, on the other hand, are very aware that they are performing. They deliver their words for maximum dramatic effect. They never throw away important lines—they savor them, underlining them verbally, putting them in bold face on the air. If you really want to capture, and hold, an audience's attention, try some of these tricks:

- If you've been speaking in a normal tone of voice and your audience is being "lulled" into too much complacency, say one important word in the next sentence in a much louder voice. If several folks act startled (like they've just awakened) repeat that last sentence for them, with a smile.

- It can be effective to start a class by telling the students you tend to talk very fast (for whatever reason—we tell them we're from New York and they seem to accept this readily as reason enough) and so it's up to them to keep you from steamrollering right over them. Tell them to wave you down if you're rolling too fast: this will inevitably become a challenge for somebody in the classroom. It has the added advantage of being a check on you, whether or not you normally do talk very fast, because when you first start to teach, you will very probably talk way too fast—nearly everyone does. You're not even aware of it. The first time we gave a presentation (using a prepared manuscript at a convention) we had practiced the talk at home and it took 40 minutes. The day we delivered it, it took 24 minutes. Whooosh!

- One of the best methods for impressing important points on an audience is to go from speaking in a normal voice to a complete stop, then repeating the point in a very low, slow voice they have to strain a little to hear. The dramatic effect underscores the information mightily. The stop before dropping your voice is essential—you want to telegraph to the audience that a change is coming, listen up. Otherwise the drop in tone can be too extreme and abrupt for them to pick up on the importance of the information, and that, after all, is your real purpose here.

- As we've noted before, there are no absolutes. Sometimes a purposeful monotone can convey your point very well, especially if you're repeating a truism, or a theory you are about to challenge in the next moment. The exaggerated monotone can inject some humor into your presentation without resorting to slapstick.

- About humor: we're not going to get into the pros and cons of incorporating humor in your teaching, because that is very much a matter of personal style, preference, and ability. But we do urge that as humorous situations arise in your classes, let it show in your voice as well as in other ways (expression, stance, etc.). It seldom hurts a presentation—and often helps—to let a class or audience know that even you, a librarian, are human; and humor can be one of the best ways to do that. The humor can be either intentional or inadvertent: we vividly remember the time, during a geology class, that a colleague mispronounced the phrase, "Bear Butte" as "bare butt." She won over an entire class with this one in about seven seconds. So laugh with the class, but never at them.

- State key points in a normal tone of voice. Pause—for a little longer than you're initially comfortable with doing, say, three seconds (three seconds is an eternity when you're giving a speech). Then lower your voice a bit and slowly repeat the point for emphasis. Many good speakers could be great speakers if they could learn to be comfortable with a little silence during their speeches. It takes confidence and experience, however, to insert pauses appropriately (and not let them become dead air space). This is a fairly sophisticated speaking technique.

These are just a few tricks we've picked up from watching good performers deliver their presentations, with a cautionary note added at the last: don't orate or overdeliver your lines. You're performing, not acting, on the classroom stage. The best advice we can give is to try to teach and present as if you were talking one-on-one to the audience, telling them a really good story. One of the best speakers we've ever heard at library-related conferences is Barbara Quint, who is able to hold meeting rooms full of hundreds of people in the palm of her hand using her expressive voice and considerable intelligence and wit. If you ever get the chance to hear her speak, we strongly urge you to go and watch what she does and think about how she does it. She has complete mastery of public speaking.

EXPRESSION

Your expressions are just as powerful in making your performance work as your voice can be. Impassivity has its place, but not very often at the front of a classroom. A professional photographer once told us that he disliked taking posed photographs, because when people were aware they were being captured by the lens their muscles froze, their complexions became waxen, and they ended up on film looking stiff and cadaverous. So he usually tried to convince clients to let him take un-posed, spontaneous photos in which people were acting naturally. We've seen inexperienced or poor public speakers take on that same waxen quality when they rose to speak: they look something like a deer frozen in the headlights.

So the best advice we can give you about your expressions is to be yourself in front of the class. That said, we should add the proviso: be yourself as soon as it's safe for you to do so. Sometimes when you're beginning to teach, your natural expressions might, well, leave a bit to be desired in terms of conveying happiness and confidence (we used to turn green before a class and the best we could manage was a very fake, sickly smile. Ugh.). If that's approximately the point you're at right now, we suggest you "try out" several safe, neutral expressions to wear until your stage fright passes—which it will. Here are a few modest suggestions (apply them to your face and features as you can):

- Calm blandness
- Interested concern
- Thoughtful consideration
- Eager anticipation
- Smiling affability

Yeah, right. This suggestion probably tears it for those of you who've been sitting the fence on just how serious we are with this stuff. But even as we offer these suggested "masks" partly in jest, we have to confess that this is a technique we've used, very successfully, in the past. When we were starting out as teachers and the panic seemed about to overwhelm us, we'd try one of these "masks" on and see how it worked. And each time, the mask got us through the rough spots. (In the early days we often waited for that crucial moment when we'd lose it completely and run out of the room. The moment never came and we never ran, and that was partly due to these masks.) It's all very well for somebody to suggest you be yourself, but until you develop a classroom persona that's comfortable and works well for you, assuming other persona can be a smart thing to do. We'll go into this more in the organizational and mental tricks to come.

BREATHING

Controlling your breathing effectively can solve most of the problems you may have experienced with public speaking. So many of the other aspects of performance are related to it: expression, voice, movement—you name it—if you're breathing properly the other stuff comes more easily. And if you're not, everything else shuts down, 'cause let's face it, the body needs its oxygen.

There are two typical kinds of breathing problems most speakers experience: hyperventilating and holding your breath. Both of them can be regulated, to a point, by the way you are speaking: short, choppy sentences may bring on hyperventilation, while long, run-on sentences may, in effect, cause you to hold your breath. And vice versa: hyperventilating may turn your sentences short and choppy, and holding your breathing may make your sentences run-on for the short term; that is, until you run out of breath and pass out. Of course you can pass out from either of these extremes, but so long as you don't fall and hit your head hard, the worst thing that's going to happen to you is just that: you'll pass out (become unconscious) for a few seconds. Then you'll come to. While you may not actively want to do this, it certainly is a more seemly reaction than say, vomiting (remember poor President Bush and the Japanese Prime Minister at the state dinner in 1992—all that videotape being edited around the world).

But c'mon, folks, that's not really likely to happen, is it? If you imagine the worst and realize it's not the end of the world, it makes it easier to cope with, doesn't it? After all, you're not likely to be embarrassing yourself before world leaders on film, are you? Gain some perspective about what's the worst that can happen and its consequences, and you'll enhance your performance abilities tenfold within minutes.

The best way to practice your breathing control is to start privately in a non-pressured, non-teaching situation. Concentrate on your breath, shut out other stimuli and think only about the breathing. Inhale slowly and exhale slowly. For optimal results, we recommend inhaling through your nose and exhaling through your mouth. As you do this, you will start to feel calmer and more relaxed.

Now, how do you manage to do this in a classroom or presentation situation when you feel like you're about to pass out from too much or too little air? There are a number of ways.

This is where having a glass or bottle of water at the podium or in the classroom can help enormously. It's perfectly understandable if a teacher or speaker needs to take a sip of water while speaking. As you go through the business of drinking a sip of water, take the opportunity to pause and concentrate on your breathing. It may be enough to get you through.

If it's not, take another pause using whatever pretexts may be at hand. If you're at a computer, minimize the screen you've been working on as if you're about to go into another system. Then maximize the screen again. Just doing this little business will give you time to concentrate on your breathing—it's familiar enough that you don't have to concentrate on commands, etc. If you're not at a computer, slowly cross from one side of the room to another (if you can be mobile), slowing your breathing down as you walk. If that doesn't work and you're standing, go to a chair at the front of the room and sit down for a minute (and conversely, if you're sitting try standing up, taking your time about shifting position and concentrating on your breathing all the while). If you are really panicked, excuse yourself for a moment, saying you'll be right back, go outside the classroom, and collect yourself. While outside the classroom, try doing some of the loosening up exercises covered previously.

These techniques have gotten us through a number of situations that, at the time, seemed insurmountable. But the thing we quickly realized about our panics was that, each time we survived one and went on, the next time it happened we were better able to handle it, having gotten through the last one. Knowing that you can—and will—get through it is the key to getting through it.

Chapter 4

MENTAL PREPARATION

Clear your mind of cant.
Samuel Johnson, From Boswell's *Life of Johnson*

The mental preparation you do for a class is different from the intellectual preparation: it's really preparing yourself emotionally for teaching (we'd have called this Emotional Preparation if we thought it wouldn't turn off a large portion of our audience . . .). Whereas we could generalize quite a bit about the physical preparations you can use in preparing to teach—since most of these can apply to everybody—we don't pretend to think that everything that works for us works for others, or vice versa, when it comes to the "windmills of the mind." So we're just going to offer a smattering of the different mental tricks we've used to make ourselves able to face the prospect of getting up and speaking in public. They are not in any particular order of importance, and they can be used selectively or as a whole package. Enjoy.

Playing Mental Tricks on Yourself
√ The "by degrees" approach
√ Role-playing
√ Coercion
√ Denial
√ Knowledge base
√ Confidence
√ Teaching is a job
√ A class is a two-way street
√ It's all public relations

THE "BY DEGREES" APPROACH

This is the most highly effective way we've found of getting ourselves to do something we absolutely cannot imagine doing. It's the basis for our organizational plan's progress, as you will see a little later. It can be devastating to imagine going from one day in which you are terrified at the prospect of teaching to the next day having to teach a class all on your own. But if you approach the same reality (one day not teaching, another, doing so) by degrees, by taking gradual steps in the process (from passive to active participation, from shared to solo responsibility) you will at the very least be able to participate in an instructional program, and in all probability, you will eventually be able to teach by yourself with confidence.

We strongly advise new teachers to go one step at a time, rather than throw themselves directly into the teaching fray—unless you have little or no performance anxiety. The reason we urge this is that we both had very bad initial experiences with public speaking: experiences that kept us from even trying to get up and speak to groups until we were quite simply told we had to do it—having no other options. This is a rotten situation in which to find oneself, and as library instructors we feel very strongly that no one should be made to do something they really don't want to do—ESPECIALLY teaching. The last thing we want in our library classrooms is people who really, really, really don't want to be there. It's the easiest way to damage both people and program; it's a lose-lose situation, a nightmare.

On the other hand, trying out different, progressively more active instructional roles in low-anxiety circumstances gives newcomers and traumatized speakers alike the safe environment they need to explore their teaching potential. Start slowly and work up to it, by degrees.

ROLE-PLAYING

One reason we suggest new teachers / speakers observe other speakers at length before doing their first presentations is so you can gather up from others the tools you'll use in your own public speaking. These tools include mannerisms, gestures, expressions, pacing, methods of emphasis—a box full of workings you can pull out of your memory and employ at will as you practice. To begin with, you may want to imitate another speaker directly, try their speaking persona on for size, see how it works for you. Don't limit yourself to trying on any one speaker's persona (would you do this when shopping for clothing? Unlikely): assume a number of different personae. We highly recommend trying out techniques and approaches that are both alien and not necessarily to your initial liking, because you may be surprised to find they can actually be tailored to fit you quite well. Experiment as much as you can with different personae until you find, adapt, and mold one into a good fit for you. At that point, you will have developed your own teaching persona.

About this whole persona idea: we know, we know, we've been telling you to be yourself. But face it: we all have both public and private selves. What we're suggesting here is that you develop a public speaking persona that is comfortable for you. The advantage this affords is that, like a favorite suit or dress, you can put it on for the class and then take it off when the class is over. This is more important than you may at first realize. As you progress in your teaching you will know what it means to be "on," that is, in your teaching persona, and you will quickly (it's to be hoped) learn the necessity of taking that persona off as soon as you can. Why? Because it can be absolutely exhausting to keep it on.

Remember, teaching is a performance—it's not day to day reality. In a class, you must maintain a level of focus, concentration, energy, and projection that you really can't keep up all the time. So develop and acknowledge your classroom persona, recognize when to put it on and when to doff it, and you will last much longer as an effective teacher.

COERCION

The success of this technique depends very much on how you react to pressure. If it makes you crazy or ineffectual, then please skip this and move on to the next tip. And please note, we've purposely specified that this is self-applied coercion only: not coercion applied by an outside agency or entity (harking back to what we said in tip #1).

But if you work well under pressure, then you certainly may be able to use this method on yourself. Tell yourself the class is something you must do and go about doing it just because you have to. Some people can make themselves do something just because they believe they should try to do it: we have seen remarkably brave performances from colleagues who were horribly frightened to speak in public, but somehow managed to make themselves do it. We admire this, but don't recommend it as a practice if it makes your life miserable. You might want to push yourself once and see how you react, but if the experience is not to your liking then please don't put yourself through hell just so you can say you made yourself do it. Once again, we refer you to the end of tip #1 in this section.

There are people who perform at their best under time pressures: a deadline makes their minds more productive, it's a challenge to get the job done at the last minute for some people. We don't recommend leaving class preparations till the last minute, at least not for new teachers. There's a difference between using pressure as a motivator and being a masochist.

DENIAL

Also known as The Scarlett O'Hara or "Fiddle-dee-dee" approach to instruction, good old denial can work like a charm for some folks. Different from the "by degrees" approach, under the denial scenario, you simply ignore the fact that you have to do the class ("I'll think about it tomorrah") until the point at which you must prepare for it. The main advantage this offers is shortening and concentrating your agonizing time (if you agonize). The main disadvantage is that it, by definition, presupposes that you are someone who operates well under pressure, and if, at that last minute, you suddenly discover that you're NOT someone who operates well under pressure, well, you're up the creek without the proverbial paddle. So use this approach with caution.

KNOWLEDGE BASE

You know more than they do. A very practical colleague of ours used to point this out to us, and she was absolutely right. The odds are that you know much more about what you're going to be teaching than anybody else in the room, except maybe your team teacher (if you have one). Remember that. Okay, so you don't know more about everything in the world than the students in your classes, but about library organization and use—trust us, you know more than they do.

You can choose to use this information in a variety of ways, both positive and negative. Awareness and acknowledgment of your knowledge base can give you the confidence simply to enter the classroom, and it can help focus your goals for the session (choosing from among the items in your knowledge base that it is essential to pass on to the students).

It can also turn you into a condescending know-it-all—unlikely, we realize, but there are varying degrees of condescension. That is, one person's insensitive reaction can come across as patronizing condescension. Why are we bringing this up? Probably because we're aware of some stereotypes flying around out there about librarians. We could choose to ignore these stereotypes, but we believe they can play a big part in our teaching, that being, our students preconceived ideas about what a library class will be like and what the librarian teaching it will be like. And one double-edged stereotype of librarians is that of the know-it-all. It is double-edged; it does make us sound intelligent and well-educated, a nice plus (and in our estimation, highly accurate). But it also works against us by putting a sour spin on our knowledge, as if we are using it as a weapon against the world. If somebody offers information in the class that you don't know, the best thing you can do is be receptive to it: welcome contributions from others. It's not an attack on you. If you treat others' contributions as an addition to the class, not only will unexpected additions not throw you but they'll make you look good, as a welcoming, open, confident person.

This kind of flexibility will reveal you as a more confident teacher (and will certainly undercut any negative stereotypes about know-it-all librarians).

Another knowledge-related stereotype that goes the rounds about librarians is that we overwhelm people with information, and when we're completely honest with ourselves, we think there is some basis for this one. When we forget to focus on the patron's needs but instead think about all there is we can give them, we can chase people away with a surfeit of our knowledge. And this is something to keep uppermost in our minds when preparing and teaching classes: teach them what they need to know, not everything we possibly can (the proverbial brain dump).

It's important to be fully aware that we are professionals with a highly-specialized, valuable body of knowledge and to go into classrooms armed with that information. It's just as important to make effective and appropriate use of our knowledge rather than to cudgel our students with our information power. As in most things, we recommend finding a good balance here.

CONFIDENCE

You've probably heard lots of people tell you that you'll develop confidence in your teaching over time, and that is true. It's the main reason we suggest practicing as much as you can: the more experience you get, the faster you gain expertise and confidence.

But what do you do to bolster your confidence from the beginning? The gradual progression we recommend you follow when starting your teaching is based on building confidence as you go along. So, too, are our suggestions for preparing class outlines, knowing the classroom and equipment, and other advance work you can do.

The bottom line about developing confidence in your teaching is to tell yourself that you can do this. We were put into positions in which we had no choice, we were told we would teach. If you're in that position too, well, like we said before, you are not alone. But if we could do it, so can you.

If you're not in the position of having to teach, the only pressure that's on you is your desire to teach. And if you have that desire, you will do it.

TEACHING IS A JOB

We tend to want to please others. We don't know if this is a tendency you share, but if it is, you may find it useful to keep in mind that teaching and presentations are jobs of work. In a job of work, you have a responsibility: to carry out the work, not to win a popularity contest. Mind you, we're not saying you shouldn't be likable, only that you should not set out merely to make a class like you. Teach them first, be fair and approachable, be yourself (your public-speaking persona self). But recognize that human nature is such that you're not going to please all the people all the time, and accept it. With some classes and students you will "connect," with others, perhaps not. But your responsibility is to deliver the information whether you like the class or not, and vice versa.

A CLASS IS A TWO-WAY STREET

Just as it's your responsibility to generate and deliver the presentation, it's the audience's responsibility to participate in the learning process. If they don't participate, if they're not receptive, if they haven't prepared properly (and by this time heaven knows *you've* prepared plenty!), they're failing to meet their part of the bargain. This is not a failure on your part.

A case in point: what about the student who falls asleep in the class? It happens. It happens in good classes, it happens in good classes with good teachers. You have no control over how much sleep that student got, when they ate lunch, whether or not they're on medication or other substances—that's their set of issues. The point is, that sleeping student is not a reflection on you and your teaching (but to be perfectly fair, ask yourself if you had lapsed into monotone . . .). That student should not be sleeping in the class. What should you do about it? First, remember to treat it as their issue, not yours. Sometimes we just ignore sleeping students: if it's a short class and their sleeping is not disruptive, we think that's the best way. In other cases, when we've had the appropriate opportunity and were not publicly singling anyone out, we've quietly asked if the student is all right (there can be serious physical reasons why a student appears to be sleeping, diabetic coma among them, so be attuned to the various possibilities and ready to call paramedics if necessary), and then suggested that the student might want to go and take a nap outside the classroom since they appear to be exhausted. We state this matter-of-factly, showing our concern rather than "outrage at their apparent repudiation of us." Like we said, it's their problem, not ours. Don't make it yours. All the responsibility does not rest on your shoulders alone.

Sometimes it's both your problem and theirs, as in the case of very early morning classes. In one such class, we had a student yawning loudly right up front. Without missing a beat, we turned to him and said, "Yep, this really IS an early class, isn't it?" The entire class immediately brightened up: both sides realized this was a less-than-ideal meeting time. This acknowledgment of a shared "adversity" quickly opened up two-way communication between the instructor and the class. If we'd simply ignored this disruption, we think the class would not have gone as well as it did—certainly the students would not have responded as openly as they did.

IT'S ALL PUBLIC RELATIONS

The last point we want to make about preparing yourself mentally for a library instruction "performance" is about the intrinsic nature of library instruction. We contend that library teaching is more of a stage performance than typical teaching. Most library teaching is a one-time-only event: you do your performance in front of your audience, and then send them into the night (or day). Although there are circumstances under which you will see your audience more than once, every library instruction session is, by its very nature, as much a public relations session as it is an instructional session.

There are many goals you may have for different library classes—ranging from basic tours to in-depth research methods—but every class, every tour, every demo, is first and last a public relations session with your clientele. Whether the class goes well or not is only partly in your hands, as we've noted above: the students and audience have a responsibility in the process just as you do. But the one thing you should emphasize in every instructional situation is that you are there to help, that your audience now has a familiar contact, a touchstone, for helping them through what can be a very daunting, challenging place. Your primary goal is to enhance the chances of their coming back and using the library effectively in the future. That goal may best be served simply by your showing them what an approachable, "regular" person you, the library teacher, are. Emphasize that being facile in using the library is not intuitively obvious: that the information landscape is shifting so fast that it can even be difficult for librarians to keep up with it. Aim at eliminating the library mystique.

Chapter 5

ORGANIZATIONAL PREPARATION: LEARNING THE BASICS AND CARRYING THEM OUT

... Art and science cannot exist but in the minutely organized particulars.

William Blake, *Jerusalem*

If you've gotten this far, you're physically and mentally prepared to start teaching. How should you begin to do it? As we've indicated earlier, we think the best way is to ease into the process gradually, and this applies both to the uninitiated (library school students and librarians who've never taught) as well as to returnees (librarians who haven't taught in a while, or who've been traumatized by hideous teaching experiences in their dark pasts—like us). The amount of time you spend on each of the steps in our progression depends on your learning style, confidence, motivation, and sense of adventure. You may decide you can eliminate one or more steps, or take them in out-of-sequence order. We suggest them in the order that seems to show a logical progression in risk-taking and responsibility.

OBSERVE OTHERS FIRST

Watch and listen to other speakers often and before you do anything else. Start out by observing those who've been recommended as outstanding to you and gradually develop your own criteria for who's good and who's not and why (and avoid making those same mistakes—make your own mistakes, not somebody else's of which

---

Learning How to Teach: The Progression

1. Observe others first
2. Take two tours of your library
3. Collaborate on a theoretical class outline
4. Keyboard or rove
5. Give a tour of your library
6. Team teach
7. Role play
8. Experiment in "safe situations"
9. Outlines and scripts
10. Gather information
11. Practice, practice, practice
12. Achieve technological competency

---

you're already aware). Take notes on techniques that don't work as well as the ones that do. Watch how good speakers move, listen to how they speak, watch to see what they do throughout the talk—where do they put their hands, what gestures do they make, how do they get important points across.

Observe some poor speakers, too, and take notes on what you see. Bad speakers are often easier to find, and it can be a lot easier to spot what they're doing badly than to zero in on exactly what it is that a good speaker does well. Once you've identified mistakes and pitfalls committed by poor speakers, avoid making the same mistakes yourself when it's your turn to perform.

Presentations, whether class or speech, are similar to good essays—they have beginnings, middles, and ends. Pay particular attention to how a good speaker begins, how they move through the phases of their presentations making smooth transitions, and how they draw the presentation to a close, just to get an idea of how to shape your own presentations. That structure works in your favor, it gives you a template to follow. Observing is the safe first step in learning how to present: you're at no risk, so take full advantage of it. And don't limit yourselves to library speakers only: there are good speakers all over the place so take 'em where you find 'em. (There's a lot to be learned from preachers and inspirational speakers, as well as professional lecturers. We've been picking up some new techniques off infomercials lately!)

TAKE TWO TOURS OF YOUR LIBRARY

A TOUR LED BY A COLLEAGUE

Taking a tour that someone else leads gives you the opportunity to see what somebody else chooses to cover about your library, as well as what they choose to leave out. We suggest that before taking the tour, as a professional courtesy, you alert the tour leader of your interest in observing their tour, just so they know a colleague will be present. This is basic good policy and etiquette.

We don't recommend you taking any active role in the tour itself at this point, unless the tour leader specifically asks you to participate or elaborate on an area within your expertise: you are there to observe. Make unobtrusive notes about the parts you'll want to keep, and on how you'll do it differently: take the good and adapt it to make it your own.

A TOUR ON YOUR OWN

Now that you have some idea of how the tours have been given at your library, take your own tour. As you walk through the building, put yourself in the place of a new user who has never been in the library before. See how easy or hard it is to find basic services and information, and plot your own future tour route out accordingly. Focus on the goals of a library tour: they are usually to highlight services and where and how users can find and get materials. Your personal tour, if taken in the mindset we're recommending, should bring out the areas that most need attention when you give a tour to others.

COLLABORATE ON A CLASS OUTLINE

This is while you're still in the pre-teaching stages. It can be very instructive to work with an experienced library teacher on an outline for a class you might someday teach or a tour you might give. Draft a plan for how you would put the class together and then give it to the experienced teacher to critique. The experienced teacher can look at your outline and tell you pretty quickly if you're trying to cover too much or too little within the time allotted to you.

Obviously, you want to work with someone you know and trust on this, someone who is knowledgeable about teaching but even more importantly, supportive of you. Sitting down and going through the step-by-step parts of a class, taking it apart and putting it back together, is a good way to prepare ahead of time for your first real class: it's a smart safety net.

KEYBOARD OR ROVE

We're on record all over the place in favor of team teaching. It was the real way we learned how to teach, and it's our favorite way of teaching still. It is much less frightening for newcomers and much more productive for expert teachers, and most importantly, it results in a better, richer class for the students—multiple teachers offer different voices and perspectives, something that can be particularly valuable for library lectures exploring different research strategies. That said, the first step we suggest in team teaching is a fairly unintimidating, low profile role, that of computer keyboarder and / or rover.

Just to clarify what their roles are: the keyboarder literally sits at the computer keyboard and types in searches while another teacher gives the actual presentation. One of the beauties of keyboarding is that it gives you the opportunity to play a larger or smaller role, depending upon your level of expertise and comfort. Early in your teaching you may not say much as the keyboarder, you may just follow the plan laid out by the presenting teacher. But as you get used to being in a semi-public role, you may find yourself offering additions and suggestions to the class as the session progresses.

Discuss the extent of your role with the presenting teacher beforehand, just so you're both clear on whether or not you might be "jumping in." Why? Because some teachers are very comfortable with others contributing to their presentations, while others are not. Surprises are not usually a good thing for anyone to get in the middle of a presentation (although most good teachers learn to handle whatever comes along). Think of this in terms of collegiality: even if you're not really team teaching yet, you are working as partners in the classroom. Lay out your game plan ahead of time so everybody knows how to proceed.

This applies to roving, as well. Roving is usually done in hands-on computer classes, when an entire classroom is set loose on the computers to do their own searches or work with various library applications and no one person can cover the entire room efficiently. So rovers move from student to student, working one on one with them to clean up computer glitches, suggest search strategies, and basically perform much in the way we all do at reference and information desks. Oftentimes, if you've keyboarded for the presentation portion of a class, as soon as the computer demo is over you're free to rove. So you're giving instruction on an individual basis.

GIVE A TOUR OF YOUR LIBRARY

If you didn't follow our suggestion of touring your library on your own, then do it now, before trying to give a tour. When you've got the major points to cover identified, run through the tour a couple of times before you actually have anyone else in tow. Why? Because on tours it's nice to have the routes (and possible alternative

---

We think tours are the best way in which anyone can "solo" perform in library instruction, for the following reasons:

√ Tours tend to be more informal, and less intimidating, than classroom instruction.

√ You can control, yet vary, the content much more easily, and it is pretty much prompted by your physical movement around the building. You're less likely to blank out during a tour when you can see service desks and other visual cues right there under your nose.

√ There're no equipment complications to worry about.

√ You can try it out on a friend—non-librarian is what we recommend—before you go live with an actual tour group. This gives you both a tabula rasa upon whom to practice AND a safe environment since you pick a friend.

---

routes) mapped out very well in your head. We've repeatedly had to take detours or cut out segments of our tours because of unannounced work going on in the building at some time or other. The more familiar you are with your route—and any possible cul de sacs or "escape routes"—the better equipped you'll be to handle exigencies.

Note Well: Be prepared to have specially-abled individuals on your tours: wheelchair-bound users, users on crutches, the hearing- and visually-impaired, and others. When we say be prepared, we mean think about how you're going to integrate them into the tour (for example, this may mean routing the tour by an elevator, rather than using the stairs as originally planned).

TEAM TEACH

For anyone who hasn't taught, or who hasn't taught much, we recommend beginning your classroom instruction experience by team teaching. This is for a number of reasons, including the most obvious one: the safety net of a partner (or as we used to think of it, misery loves company). And for those of you who are appalled that we've used the word misery, we assure you it's not lightly or flippantly chosen. For us, the first few classes were pretty miserable. We didn't have anybody telling us anything about how to go about it. It was a wholly inimical enterprise for us: we're both basically very private individuals. It wasn't easy to go into the classroom at first.

But there were also very practical reasons for us taking to team teaching. We were giving lots of introductory classes in using the new online public catalog at the time, at first doing demonstrations only and then in hands-on, interactive classes in a large electronic classroom. It made sense for us to team-teach these classes: one of us would be at the keyboard, the other would lecture (although sometimes the one at the keyboard would also lecture, and the other teacher would jump in as needed and then rove during the interactive portion of the class).

None of us involved in the instructional program had much teaching experience to begin with, so we developed a working plan for these classes and then fine-tuned them as we went along. Having two people in the room divided the intellectual responsibility (which turned out to be useful later on in the life of the instructional program for bringing in new people who lacked confidence—it helped them build it when teaching with more seasoned performers) and divided the workload, which is an appreciable consideration for the kinds of library classes we typically teach now and are likely to be teaching in the foreseeable future. If you're teaching more than six or eight people at a time in a hands-on class, you'd better wear rollerblades if you have no team teacher or rover working with you. Or, if you're teaching a class that involves both printed and electronic resources, it can be a good idea for one person to present the print and the other to present the electronic, with each chiming in as you go.

So team teaching works well in just about any combination: two greenhorns, one experienced teacher and a new recruit, or two old hands working together. And think about it, the students benefit a great deal from having two teachers in the classroom: it's double the knowledge and information available to them. Imaginative pairings of teachers can also create dynamite teams: We discovered that a team consisting of a public services librarian and a technical services librarian brought about lots of win-win situations, because both played to their strengths. The knowledge about the catalog that the tech service librarian brought to the class made these sessions learning experiences for both students and their team teacher alike, whereas the public services librarian's knowledge of information-seeking behaviors gave their tech services teammate a new perspective on how to teach. Team teaching is the most overlooked potential staff team-building tool of which we know. It's hard to imagine a better way to get different library service units to understand better what the other guy does and to work towards a common goal than to put members of those units into a classroom together to teach.

Some people have registered concern about the time and workload implications of team-teaching: they raise the issue of using two instructors for one class as a negative one. We can only point out that, in our experience, it's a heckuva lot easier, and better, to team-teach four classes than to solo teach two. It's less physically and emotionally demanding, and we, as instructors, believe we deliver better classes when we team teach. Certainly the feedback from students has supported this belief.

There are two other huge benefits that come from team teaching: one is related to the safety net issue, the other to instructional evaluation. When you team teach with another librarian, you are both putting yourselves on the line. That means both people are taking the same public speaking risk. If this sounds off-putting, take a moment to consider what this really means. You're both in that classroom to do the class, with equal responsibility. You're a team. If one of you is having an off-day (and we all do), in a well-functioning team the other person can carry the ball and take up the slack. If you're both "on" that day, you can create an interpersonal dynamic that will really energize the entire classroom. If you get a question that "rattles" or nonpluses one of you, the other can often jump in and "save your team bacon." Each way, the students—and teachers—come out ahead.

If one of you is a less effective teacher, that person can learn from the one with more expertise. We've had expert teachers emerge from behind the keyboard after a few sessions of working with glib speakers: initially they felt safest with the technology, but after "seeing how it's done" they couldn't sit still any more—they came to the front of the classroom and helped with examples and explanations. This has even happened with librarians who've been observing classes; we refer to it as the "suck them in and turn them on" method of helping colleagues learn to teach. Get a librarian into a classroom, touch on their area of expertise, and nine times out of ten they're going to have some good information to volunteer for the class, or enhanced knowledge that "must be shared." It's a mere hop and a step from adding a comment to going up front and telling the students more . . . and another new instructor is sucked into the fold . . . yes!

Now about the instructional evaluation benefit. Listen up carefully to this one, because assessment and evaluation are two hot hot hot terms being applied to library instruction right now. Why? We don't know. It's no more or less important than it's ever been. We figure it's a buzzword that came up in a conference somewhere recently and caught on. In any case, we're all for it because the quality of library instruction can vary a great deal, and librarians themselves have the ability to improve their teaching if they stay open and receptive to learning while they teach.

Evaluation of any kind is a highly sensitive issue, and it's especially sensitive for new teachers who may be, well, sensitive about their performance. There's no better way to turn off new instructors than for them to be given overly-critical, non-constructive feedback about their early performances. Trust us, we've been there. Empty praise is not the answer, but neither is potentially ego-destroying criticism.

When you are learning to teach, what better way to begin the on-going evaluation of your teaching than by co-self-evaluating your team-taught sessions? This does not mean automatic patting of each other on the backs; neither does it mean nitpicking each other's performance apart. You're both on the line here, remember? What we have done—and it works very, very well—is hold debriefing sessions immediately after classes. The team teachers sit down after the class (it doesn't have to be for long, 15 to 20 minutes can do the trick) and, using non-weighted language, talk about what worked well and what needs to be changed in the class.

We think the advantage to this kind of assessment is obvious: it's the teachers themselves putting themselves on the line, rather than uninvolved third parties. It's an immediate reality check, as well as a ready means of improving your teaching ("here's what worked, now let's change what didn't seem to go over so well"). If the purpose of evaluation and assessment are to improve performance—and that's our understanding of them—then co-self-assessment is an excellent method to use.

This assessment technique is not just for new teachers: it can be used very productively throughout your teaching career, and we recommend it. It can refocus you

SIDEBAR

What We Mean by "Non-weighted Language"

Non-weighted language is saying something in language that doesn't contain heavy value judgments. Telling someone after a class that, "You were really good," or "You were really bad," doesn't give them much actual feedback about what they did and how effective it was (and depending upon which one of these you use, may drive that teacher out of the classroom forever). We're talking about using tact, yes, but it's more than that: it's giving your colleagues (and your colleagues giving YOU, remember) objective feedback that addresses what they did, not who they are.

Non-weighted feedback focuses on techniques and behaviors in light of how well they worked. For example: "When you first gave the explanation of subject headings, I observed that several students appeared confused. When you repeated the explanation using slightly different wording, and demonstrated how the headings work in the OPAC, I observed those same students indicating understanding."

Another example from a team-teaching session: "I think it would be more effective for us to do a short online demonstration and then a tour rather than to focus on hands-on work for the next class we do like this. The students showed a reasonable understanding of the online tools, but their questions indicated they don't know their way around the library and its services."

And another example of what can come up in a debriefing: "It's my perception that we may be trying to cover too much material in this class: the students seemed rushed through the hands-on portion. I'd like us to go over the class outline and re-evaluate just what we're really trying to teach and focus on those points for the next class of this type."

Even when you are giving feedback about a teacher's personal characteristics, there are ways of wording the feedback that keep it from becoming a personal attack. For someone who has spoken inaudibly in a class, you can offer the observation, "It appeared that some people in the back of the room were having difficulty hearing the lecture. Next time it may work better to face the class more and direct your voice toward the students more often."

We're expressing these comments in highly formal language for publication purposes: your own discussions will doubtless be more informal. But please note some of the phrases we've used: "I observed," "I think," and "It's my perception." Your perceptions are just that: your perceptions. They are not right, or wrong, or the law. Each of these phrases opens up a dialogue for discussion between the team teachers, but does not attack or degrade any of the participants involved. This kind of language communicates mutual respect between members of the teaching team—and that is one of the inestimable rewards about being part of a team.

when you stray in your presentations, and it can revitalize you when you feel burn-out coming on. It's one of the main reasons we are so enthusiastic about team teaching.

ROLE-PLAY

When you're first starting out, role playing can get you farther, faster than just trying to be yourself. We know we brought it up before, but we're reiterating it here because we think you should keep this in mind as a technique to use when team teaching.

You're all familiar with the concept of "good cop-bad cop," right? Well, when we were teaching a library research course with a colleague long ago, on the first day of class one of us would be good cop and one of us bad cop. One of us would play the heavy, laying down the law of the course syllabus, emphasizing how much work was involved and making our high expectations clear. And when we asked if anyone wanted to bail out after getting a clearer picture of what the reality was, sometimes one or two students would elect to do so. After their exit, the other one of us would talk about the first assignment, making it clear that we were there to help and guide the students, and, that as long as they showed up for class and made an effort, they had nothing to worry about.

Our goal was to discourage those students from taking the course who were just looking for a "gut credit" (tourists, as our colleague privately characterized them) while retaining students who actually wanted to learn how to do library research. This strategy successfully gave the tourists and non-tourists a taste of class reality. (Please note: the course was always overenrolled, which is why we were concerned about whom we enrolled. We figured it made better sense to let in the students who might actually show up throughout the term rather than those who would drop when they realized they had to work.) But we digress . . . .

The point of this story is that playing "good cop-bad cop" gave us excellent opportunities for role playing because we'd switch roles from term to term. And in teaching the course with other colleagues, as we sometimes did, we'd use the same kind of role playing. Not only did it yield classes of students who learned how to do library research, but it gave the instructors the opportunity to explore different instructional persona. Those personae have come in handy over the years considering the variety of teaching and presentation circumstances in which we've found ourselves.

EXPERIMENT IN "SAFE SITUATIONS"

Now that we've given our disquisition on team teaching, we have much less to cover in this section because we think we've delineated a number of the situations in which you might want to experiment: While team teaching with someone you trust, swapping off different roles with your teaching teammates is an ideal time. You can experiment in big ways and little ways. We remember the time a colleague brought a beach ball to class and tossed it back and forth with the students, the idea being to illustrate the "back and forth" dynamic between student and teacher. Everyone was a little taken aback, but it did perk up the proceedings and did no one any permanent damage (it was an inflatable beach ball).

We prefer to experiment on a smaller scale: trying out new ways of beginning the class, using different examples and metaphors, sometimes asking students in the class to keyboard for the computer demo—that kind of thing. If you are going to experiment on a larger scale, we'd advise not committing your whole presentation to the experiment. That way, if the experiment fails (and they do, and you learn from it, so don't let the prospect of failure intimidate you) you can still accomplish the main goals of the class.

A few words more on failure: keep the failures in perspective. If you do your preparation sufficiently and then experiment with a presentation rationally (e.g., the ways we suggest), you're not likely to BOMB. You may do a quiet flop. And it's after these presentations that debriefing sessions are most valuable: you'll be grateful for the opportunity to compare horror stories, get the reactions out of your systems, and thus recover. If we'd had the wit in the early days to purge ourselves of the flops at the time they happened, we wouldn't have wasted time and energy carrying around so much rotten emotional baggage about public speaking. When you flop while team teaching, you flop together. And you can pick up the pieces together, too.

If you do a real stinkeroo of a class all by yourself, then instead of just feeling lousy afterward, give yourself your very own personal debriefing and ask yourself the same kinds of questions you'd ask in a team debriefing session: *and ask them of yourself in the same way that you'd ask others.* This last part is key, because we all tend to be harder on ourselves than on others, and you're likely to start calling yourself names if you give in to your initial feelings. Don't. Treat yourself with the same respect and tact you'd give others after a bad experience: be supportive of your own teaching and remember that this was just one class, not the end of the world or of your successful teaching. Then go over in your mind what went right, what went wrong, and fix it for next time out. Don't hesitate to talk with others you trust if you need some help at this point—it can help you maintain a healthy perspective, learn how to correct your mistakes, and not get down in the dumps.

OUTLINES AND SCRIPTS

We'll talk about how we go about putting these together in much more detail in Part 2, but right now we'd like just to get you thinking about which of these formats might work well for you on various speaking occasions.

An OUTLINE (sometimes we also call it a CLASS PLAN) gives the major points you're going to be covering during a presentation and shows the progression of the class with some details (sample searches you plan to use, for example). It may outline the broader parts of the class (for example, a computer demonstration, hands-on work, covering printed resources, a tour). It may also contain the list of databases and print resources you'll be covering, as well as the specific searches and examples you plan to use in your demonstrations. It may contain classroom "choreography" if you are team teaching and plan to divide responsibilities between instructors (A does this, B does that). If one person is keyboarding and the other is lecturing, it may be useful for a class outline to include the step-by-step searches you will be doing (as much as you may like surprises the rest of the time, it can be time-consuming and frustrating not to work out effective practice searches ahead of time—it doesn't make sense to spend 10 minutes of a 50 minute class groping for a search that illustrates the point you're trying to make). You'll make up most of the actual wording and fill in the details as you go along, but your presentation follows the outline's progression.

When to use an outline: We make up class outlines for every class we do. They vary considerably in length and detail, however. For our recurring OPAC introductions, the class outline often consists of just sample searches. For in-depth, subject-specialized classes, the class outline can run to several pages. We've used outlines successfully in public presentations as well. If you're doing a presentation in an area you've never done before, you may want to make up an extensive outline (or use the script method we present below). If you're using presentation software (like Microsoft PowerPoint) you'll pretty much want to do it in outline form (more on this later).

When not to use an outline: We honestly can't think of any situation when it would hurt to do a class outline. That's because we figure that no matter how many times we've taught a particular class, it's always a good thing to update our preparation. Case in point: when teaching many online resources, timeliness is an issue. So we update our class outlines for classes that include these resources to coax out the most recently released materials to illustrate their immediacy. Keep in mind that flexibility is key to good teaching; so if, during a class, you realize you need to deviate from the class outline—DO!

On the other hand, if you're doing a public presentation to a very large audience and you're really nervous about it, use the script method rather than the outline. Later on we'll give you some tips for how to work effectively from a script (putting some "oomph" into it) and if you're really wigged-out about facing a large audience, the last thing you need to worry about is your mind going blank and all you have is an outline. There are times when it's a good thing to have the words right there in front of you to read.

A SCRIPT is pretty much a word-for-word version of the presentation you're going to make. You read from it.

When to use a script: We work from scripts when we are doing public speeches, when we have a set number of minutes to talk, and when questions, if any, will come at the end of the speech in response to it. Examples of these occasions include beginning-of-term orientation sessions and library conferences.

When not to use a script: During a class. We've tried using a script for a class ("Good morning. My name is "YOUR NAME HERE" . . .) and have found it limp and uninformative at best, and mind-bendingly boring and claustrophobic at worst. If you're counting on following a script and someone asks a question, it will throw you off entirely. If you prepare yourself reasonably well for the class, you will be able to handle the spontaneous questions.

Which of these methods will work best for you? The only way you can know is by trying them out in various situations. We've experimented with them all for a variety of reasons, some unintentional. There was the first presentation we made at a national conference when one of us had prepared detailed index cards of information (pretty much a script) as well as an overhead transparency of an outline of the talk. As we stepped forward to the podium, all the index cards fell out of our hands onto the floor. Scrambling all over the front of the room to pick them up didn't seem like the thing to do at the moment, so we "wung it" using the outline. We should point out that the reason we were able to wing it working just from the outline was because we'd prepared so much on those cards, but you'll be surprised what you can actually do in a pinch ("Necessity yadda yadda yadda invention . . . ").

GATHER INFORMATION

The sooner you get good and adept at this the better. It's as basic to instruction as a good reference interview is to reference service, and they happen to have a lot in common because what you're doing in both instances is gathering information.

A good class delivers the instruction that's needed to the students as close as possible to the time when they need it. So when you are setting a class up, you want to get those basic journalistic questions answered first (who, what, when, where, how, and why) and then go into greater detail in filling in the why. This applies to the regular instructional sessions you may schedule as part of your library instruction program (regular classes in using the OPAC or Web-based resources, for example), to subject-related classes you do at the request of others, and to credit-bearing library classes. You need to know who the target audience is, what the class is about, when and where the class is going to be given, how you're going to go about teaching it, and why the class is being given (get a syllabus and any library-related assignments from an instructor in advance of the class whenever possible). Sometimes you are developing classes in response to a perceived need and you will be the one generating the answers to those questions. At other times, you'll need to pull this information out of someone else who is asking you to do a class or training session. But the more you know about your audience (what their level of library and computer expertise is, what the subject area they're working in is, whether there are special language or ability needs, etc.) and what their expectations are for the class, the better you can prepare to meet those expectations.

Remember us mentioning "flops" a little while ago? Most of the flops with which we've been associated in our careers came from a mismatch between what the audience expected and what the instructors delivered; and that was not due to bad teaching, it was due to poor communication in the information-gathering before the class. The good thing about making such a flop is you learn very quickly not to do it a lot, because it's usually painfully evident when such a flop is in progress: you lose their attention fast. Always target your teaching at the audience's need, and to do that you first have to know what it is they need.

PRACTICE

If you're not at least a little tired of hearing us say this by now, we feel we've failed; because we just can't say it too much. To improve your teaching, you've got to practice a lot. If you go into the classroom once or twice a year, you may "get through," but it's highly doubtful you're going to be really effective. It takes practice to achieve expertise in any endeavor, and with library teaching, considering the rate of change in library systems and resources, it takes lots of ongoing work to maintain it.

If it's not feasible for you to get up in front of a library class that often, there are other avenues you can use to hone your teaching skills. We taught one-on-one at the reference desk for years before we devoted our lives to instruction. We teach colleagues how to use library office applications one-on-one and in small to large groups. Putting together an effective handout on how to search a database or find a book in the stacks is a printed form of library instruction, and uses the same organizational and visual presentation skills you'd use in a class.

Go outside the library to gain experience and confidence. Join Toastmasters in your local community. Take a public speaking class in an adult education program. At academic institutions, it's often possible to have yourself videotaped while doing a presentation—take advantage of this opportunity, and, if possible, have a professional presenter critique the tape with you.

Or you can do a lot on your own, in the privacy of your home or office. Write an explanatory speech on how to tie a shoelace; the practice in describing a simple, yet involved, step-by-step process such as this gives you excellent preparation for thinking through a class outline. Practice reading aloud, first to yourself, then to (trusted) others. Read poetry, plays, news stories, or ghost or horror stories. Read material that will stretch the emotional tones of your voice and delivery pace. You'll be surprised at how this private preparation can help you perform in public. For one thing, you'll get used to hearing the sound of your own voice.

Teaching is a state of mind as much as it is being up in front of the classroom. You can maintain that state of mind in a variety of ways—so make good use of them.

ACHIEVE TECHNOLOGICAL COMPETENCY

There are more things to practice, practice, practice than just getting up in front of the room and speaking or teaching. One of the key things you want to be adept at is any technology you might be using in classes. This includes knowing your way around hardware, software, and your network sufficiently so you can at least make your way in and out of the systems you'll be using and troubleshoot the basic glitches that are likely to occur. Practice starting the system, using the applications you'll be teaching with, and getting out. If you're teaching in an electronic classroom, familiarize yourself with the various components in it: the teaching station, individual workstations, any broadcasting or control systems, the LCD projector, presentation software—whatever you'll be using in class. If you familiarize yourself with nothing else in a classroom in which you'll be giving a computer demonstration, make sure you have the name and phone number of whomever you call in the event the system goes down. Technological competency is another incentive for team teaching: You can learn about equipment from a more experienced person, the two of you can put your heads together to solve crises, or one of you can do the chalk talk (see below for more on this) while the other tries to get the system up and running.

Chapter 6

PERFORMANCE TEMPO

Each honest calling, each walk of life, has its own elite,
its own aristocracy based on excellence of performance.
James Bryant Conant, *Our Fighting Faith,*
"In This Country There Are No Classes"

Up till now, we've talked about how to prepare in advance for making a presentation. But there are certain things you will need to take care of a day or two before the presentation (when possible) or on the day of the presentation itself. We want to make you aware of these things, too. Here's our checklist:

> √ Check your appearance in a mirror
>
> √ Get there well ahead of time
>
> √ Immediately scope out the room
>
> √ Meet and know thy equipment
>
> √ Have visual backup
>
> √ The chalk talk
>
> √ Be ready for Murphy's Law
>
> √ When glitches arise, let others know what happened

CHECK YOUR APPEARANCE IN A MIRROR

Why? Well, of course, you want to look neat and tidy going up in front of a group. And also because it can be incredibly distracting to the class if you have inadvertently tucked your dress up into your pantyhose, have a piece of spinach stuck in your teeth, or are trailing a long piece of toilet paper off the sole of your shoe. And, if you think we're making this up, think again. We've done or seen all of these situations, and have witnessed even more outlandish things (that we're not gonna list here) happening to instructors.

GET THERE WELL AHEAD OF TIME

If it's your first time using a certain classroom, and the room is onsite (at your institution), go into it and look around well before the class or session and run through the rest of this checklist. If the classroom in which you're going to be presenting is offsite (in another library or city), try to arrange to get into the room the day—or at least an hour (or as close to it)—before your presentation and run through the rest of this checklist.

Why is it so important to get there ahead of time? Well, the most immediate reason is that it's a bad idea for you to run into a room at the last minute, puffing, just before you have to get up and speak. The other reasons involve familiarizing yourself with the tools you'll be using.

IMMEDIATELY SCOPE OUT THE ROOM

Scope out the room and get comfortable with it. Check lighting, temperature, amplification, and choreograph your positions. If you can influence all of these aspects of the room environment, by all means do so, since they all will affect your performance. We've talked about room temperature and positioning before; by getting into the room well before the presentation you can block out where you should position yourself and check out the room's temperature, as well as lighting and microphone controls (some rooms have this last, others don't). Be prepared for contingencies under which you will have control over only some, or even none, of these environmental and spatial considerations: lots of classrooms have no in-room thermostat, or the lighting controls are only two choices (off and on), or there is no microphone, or there is only one place from which you can teach. It's still better for you to scope this out before you go on, so you can make whatever possible adjustments and accommodations in your presentation you can devise.

MEET AND KNOW THY EQUIPMENT

The ideal situation lets you try out the equipment at least a day in advance of the class. If at all possible, at least try it out a half hour before your presentation. We covered much of this in an earlier section, but it's worth repeating here: Make sure the computers you'll be using are working before you start teaching.

HAVE VISUAL BACKUP

The experienced teacher metaphorically wears suspenders and a belt while teaching. That is, veteran instructors have visual backup plans for their classes. This may include canned computer presentations (for when the network goes down), overhead transparencies (for when the computers crash), handouts (when even the electricity fails), and the last example in this list, which you should be prepared to do for any class:

THE CHALK TALK

First thing, make sure there's a chalkboard and chalk, a white board and grease pens, or a flip chart and marker, available in the room. Because, if all the computers crash and the overhead fails, you may end up doing "the chalk talk" on the board: literally writing out various computer commands and search strategies you would normally show online. This one is but a step away from shadow puppets, but we've done more of them in our careers than you might expect. What usually happens is the system goes down temporarily and you do a partial chalk talk while you're waiting for it to come back. Hey, it beats shadow puppets, folks.

BE READY FOR MURPHY'S LAW

We've tried to give you the benefit of everything we can think of that you may be able to anticipate for preparing your performance. But you know the truth of Murphy's Law: Anything that can go wrong WILL go wrong. There are the proverbial "acts of god" which take place that are entirely outside your control: power grids fail, fire alarms go off, the network server crashes. You cannot keep any of these things from ever happening.

So, if you have a little spot in the back of your subconscious that is aware of this on some level, when it happens it won't hit you like a ton of bricks; it'll be somewhat expected. Acknowledge to yourself that everything will not run perfectly, and deal with the problems as they come along.

WHEN GLITCHES ARISE, LET OTHERS KNOW WHAT HAPPENED

One last bit of advice to keep you and your instructional colleagues sane: If you do encounter technological problems with equipment or network resources during a class, in addition to reporting the problem to your systems support people, let others who may be teaching know about it. If you have a head instructor or coordinator of instruction, notify them so that the information can be distributed and instructors can revise their class plans as necessary.

Part Two

COMPOSING CLASSES

Chapter 1

A BASIS UPON WHICH TO BUILD

Beware lest you lose the substance by grasping at the shadow.

Aesop, *The Dog and the Shadow*

From the amount of time we've spent thus far talking about performing tricks, tips, and techniques, we may have given the impression that it doesn't much matter what you say in the classroom, just how you say it. Nothing could be further from the truth. Although self-confidence and an effective presentation style get you in the door and started on your journey, you won't get far if you don't deliver the appropriate message. Without good content, what's the point of doing a tour, class, demonstration, or presentation at all? Having said that, we obviously cannot address the specifics of exactly what you will teach, since it will vary enormously from library to library. We can, however, sketch out some approaches for how to deliver a variety of library messages: public relations presentations, one-shot general information classes, subject-specific orientations, and more.

So the second part of this book is devoted to The Message: How we identify it, how we articulate and demonstrate it, and how to ensure that we're sending it clearly. Being children of the 60s, this sounds to us like a good time to define our philosophy of library instruction.

TWO JOURNEYWOMEN'S PHILOSOPHY OF LIBRARY INSTRUCTION

Although unlikely to rival Ranganathan's Laws of Library Science in the annals of library history, our instructional philosophy is pretty much summed up by these Basic Five Tenets (If these sound hauntingly familiar we wouldn't be surprised—they're an amalgamation of our thoughts, the wisdom of George M. Cohan, and a tad of Sir Isaac Walton's *The Compleat Angler*):

Basic Tenet #1: Know more than they do, but don't rub it in.

Basic Tenet #2: Put yourself in the student's place (remember that dim and distant time before library school when you didn't know more about libraries than they do?).

Basic Tenet #3: The goal of the library class is to make it easier for patrons to use the library.

Basic Tenet #4: If a person wants a fish, get them to the fish (or get the fish to them) as quickly as possible.

Basic Tenet #5: Leave them wanting more, not less.

We're tempted just to leave it at that, since neither of us is really big on philosophizing, but it might be useful to follow our own advice and ensure that we are articulating our message. So here's what the Tenets mean to us:

BASIC TENET #1: KNOW MORE THAN THEY DO, BUT DON'T RUB IT IN.

Okay, so maybe in the grand scheme of things you don't know more about *everything* than your users do (we did toy with the idea of a Basic Tenet #6, "Don't be so literal-minded," but decided it was unnecessary. Don't make us regret this decision). There will certainly be people in your classroom who know much more than you do about various subjects and disciplines, perhaps about electronic resources, maybe even the Web, public policy, data crunching, or conspiracy theories . . . (you see how this list can go on if you let it?).

Don't dwell on how expert *they* are in their fields, although you should certainly acknowledge that they have their specialties just as you have yours. The fact that they are in a library classroom puts them on *your* playing field. And surely you will concede that you probably know more about library research and the workings of your library and its collections than most, if not all, of the people sitting in your library class, including classroom faculty. This is one of your bases of power in the library classroom—depend upon it, cherish it, be confident in it. It works much better for getting up in front of groups than imagining everyone in their underwear (an image that usually distracts us so much, if we conjure it up, we can't teach anymore). You do know more about library stuff than the patron does.

But let's go back and underline one of those basic life rules Mom and Dad taught us as they sent us out to the playground: Just because you have confidence (are bigger, stronger, smarter, whatever), you shouldn't boast or swagger or lord it over others. Translated into library instruction settings, this means show confidence, but don't talk down to the class. Don't patronize them just because you know the library stuff better than they do. There are no stupid questions when you're first learning something. Surely you've been in a class at sometime in which you were totally at a loss. What were you most afraid of? Looking stupid in front of the rest of the class. Ever see someone belittle somebody else for asking a question? Remember how you felt about said belittler? Especially if you were the one being belittled? The attitude you convey in front of the class is crucial. As a teacher you are in a position of power, use it for the good of the library and the profession. Whether or not you subscribe to our belief that 90 percent of library instruction is public relations, those of you who have ever taught will probably acknowledge the fact that library instructors who can convey a sense of receptivity, discovery, and eagerness to learn along with the rest of the class make the best teachers.

BASIC TENET #2: PUT YOURSELF IN THE STUDENT'S PLACE (REMEMBER THAT DIM AND DISTANT TIME BEFORE LIBRARY SCHOOL WHEN YOU DIDN'T KNOW MORE ABOUT LIBRARIES THAN THEY DO?).

The implied phrase that ends Basic Tenet #2 is, "and teach accordingly." If we can convince you of nothing else in this book, please internalize the necessity for librarians to remember what it's like walking into a place where you know none (or few) of the rules but have to learn how to play the game. So walk around your library in a patron's—a novice, first-time-in-the-door patron's—shoes and don't be surprised if you see your services and collections in an entirely new light. Put your library skills classes together keeping in mind what you learn on such a walk-through.

Having mastered the mysteries of classification systems, stack charts, OPACs, compact shelving, and library jargon, it's very easy for us librarians to forget that patrons may have no idea of what we're talking about when we tell them to "search the online catalog and electronic databases for citations to monographs and periodicals arranged in the stacks according to LC classification." Online catalog? Database? Citations? Whuh?

Let's face it, in libraries we don't talk like normal people. We speak a highly specialized language. We sling the library lingo around (and heaven forbid that we lapse into fluent acronym). This is one of the easiest pits into which any library instructor falls: to forget the difference between our experience and that of the class. One of the fastest, and easiest, ways to lose an entire classroom of perfectly intelligent adult learners is to overwhelm them with the jargon. Some folks use library jargon in a way that manages to violate Basic Tenets #1, #2, #3, and #5. They use it to confuse and impress rather than to pave the way for better understanding of how the library works.

Effective teachers use illustrative examples and explain jargon along the way. They share their knowledge with users rather than use it as a barrier separating "us" from "them." Library teachers who hide behind library language merely reveal their lack of confidence and inexperience. This is an area in which we all need constant vigilance and renewal because it's just as easy to use jargon thoughtlessly as it is to do it intentionally. We usually start our classes by asking students to "keep us honest" at the outset. We tell the class to question any acronym or term we may fling at them that's not clear and assure them that when this happens it's our problem in communicating, not their shortfall for learning. And that's true.

BASIC TENET #3: THE GOAL OF THE LIBRARY CLASS IS TO MAKE IT EASIER FOR PATRONS TO USE THE LIBRARY.

If more libraries were designed with this same goal in mind, we library instructors would have much less work to do. But architects' aesthetics often carry more weight in the design of libraries than the mere notion that the layout should make the place easy and intuitively obvious to use. As long as this practice continues, we're gonna have plenty of work to do making up for the deficiencies aesthetics can create.

As library instructors it's our task to convey information that makes patrons more effective in using the library, because the patron's goal is to get what they want from the library (not to become expert librarians themselves). This goal is sometimes easy to lose sight of while we're concentrating on either macrocosmic goals (critical thinking, information literacy, and the research process, for example) or microcosmic goals (Boolean searching of online databases, for example) of our own. The patron needs to use the library for their purposes, not ours. The trick is to provide both the information and an appropriate context in which the patron can make her/his choices about how the information will be used.

BASIC TENET #4: IF A PERSON WANTS A FISH, GET THEM TO THE FISH (OR GET THE FISH TO THEM) AS QUICKLY AS POSSIBLE.

Sometimes a person just wants the fish—and sometimes we have to teach them the shortest, fastest way to get the fish rather than the best or most effective way to get it (this is one of the harder tenets for most of us to swallow, and, indeed, we argue between ourselves over this one). But we do accept as a basic tenet that the patron's goal is often to find the information, materials, or data they are seeking as quickly as possible in order to do something else in their lives, rather than learn how to fish for it expertly (the research process). So instead of elegant fly-casting, one may have to use the Ronco portable reel method in teaching.

BASIC TENET #5: LEAVE THEM WANTING MORE, NOT LESS.

This is the most basic premise of showmanship. Dump too much on them and you lose them for life—they flee at your approach and never come near a reference desk or possibly even a library again. Leave them with a sense that there is more you can give, and either they come back to find it or move on unharmed—untraumatized by information overload.

Okay, so we've got this philosophy. Where do we go from here? How do we use it to create classes? There are a number of ways you may proceed to put a class, workshop, tour, demo, or training together. Since we've already revealed that we like to plan ahead for every class, the first thing we want to cover is the Class Outline. Think of this outline as a map of your teaching strategy.

Chapter 2

PREPARING THE CLASS OUTLINE

A mighty maze! but not without a plan.
Alexander Pope, *An Essay on Man*

For the first few classes you're preparing, we suggest the following formula for drawing up the class outline:

√   Create Draft 1 of Class Outline

√   Draft 1 Class Outline – 1/2 = Draft 2 Class Outline

√   Draft 2 Class Outline – 1/3 = End Result (1/3rd original outline)

In English, this formula should be read thusly: prepare a draft outline of the class you think you want to teach. When you've prepared that outline, go back and review it and cut it in half. (This will be like pulling your own teeth the first few times you attempt it because there is SO much to teach them! SO much valuable information! Never mind . . . pull those teeth.)

At this point, you've got a class outline that is about half of what you were first determined to teach. Now, go back over this new outline and cut it by one-third. This will either be much easier the second time around because the first revision was so painful, or it may be like a do-it-yourself amputation if your first outline was so overblown that it wasn't all that hard to cut away half of it. In any case, pare the outline down by a third.

You should now have a class outline that is approximately 1/3rd the size of your original plan, and, for most of us starting out, that's a realistic amount of material to

---

☛ **Insider Teaching Tips**

Throughout this chapter, we're going to insert a number of Insider Teaching Tips. These are some highly specific suggestions for techniques to use in classes once you've gained some instructional confidence. They are suggestions only, you will develop your own personal techniques as you teach. But we've found these approaches useful in making classes a little more interesting or taking them out of the ordinary. Usually they serve as catalysts to stimulate the class.

---

keep after revision. New teachers (ourselves very much included once upon a time) tend to try to cover way too much, mostly for the noblest of motives: enthusiasm for the subject and a strong mission to convey information.

Unfortunately, the typical one-shot, 50-minute instructional session does not allow you enough time to successfully impart everything they need to know, let alone everything you WANT them to know. Studies routinely show that people ultimately retain only a "residue" of about 5 percent of a lecture.[1] Although some of you may interpret this to mean that you should therefore teach them a whole lot, in the interests of their retaining more overall—it doesn't work that way, folks. Similar studies indicate that the best teaching focuses on a few key points and emphasizes and re-emphasizes them throughout the class. [2] [Remember Sherlock Holmes' contention that once your brain reaches capacity, for every new fact you stuff in another falls out.] So if you're planning to teach the spectrum of information literacy in one 50-minute class—think again. Start out with a simple outline and build from there.

WHAT GOES INTO THE OUTLINE

There are a few elements you should cover in each and every class. They include:

1. Welcome them to the library—ALWAYS!
2. Introduce yourself and tell them what you do. (Not just a title, but give them context: "I teach classes for the sociology department in using the library"; "I teach and work at the reference desk"; "I buy the materials for the philosophy collections in the library.")
3. Tell them what you're going to teach them.
4. Teach them (cover the "meat" of the class).
5. Review (tell them what you just taught them).
6. Tell them how to reach you and/or your colleagues for help in the future.
7. Thank them for coming.

Let's go over these elements in detail and expand on what we mean.

THE WELCOME

It's good manners to acknowledge that they are guests and you are their host or hostess. And it's a good way to start. It breaks the ice and helps students perceive you as a human being rather than as an anonymous entity. And it segues into the next step: introducing yourself.

INTRODUCTIONS

Always introduce yourself, not just as a matter of form but so students can put you in context. Tell them enough about yourself so they can understand why it is you are teaching the class. During this "introduction," you may want to establish any connection you may have with the subject or with the class instructor, or you may want to poll the group (always trying to get as much information about your audience as possible). For example, you may want to ask how many of them have already used the library, how many of them know how to do subject searching of the OPAC, or if they all know what a URL is.

Frame your questions to get a sense of just what level of student you're working with. Even though at this point you will have a class outline, remember what we said about being flexible. After getting answers to your questions, you may want to make a few adjustments in your class outline. Typically, you may decide to cover even less than you originally planned. You may add more databases, or change the ones you plan to search, based on what the class or instructor tells you during this introductory phase. But ask some questions right up front, it gives you a basis from which to work and it helps establish some rapport with the class.

This is also a good time to warn the class about yourself—that is, tell them not to let you get away with using any jargon or unfamiliar and sinister initials that they don't know. Warn them that you, as a librarian, tend to do this and cannot help yourself, but that it's their duty to keep you from lapsing into "libraryese." This, too, can establish a nice rapport with the class, makes you look human and approachable, and usually gives them a great deal of incentive to listen carefully to what you're saying.

TELLING THEM WHAT YOU'RE GOING TO TEACH THEM

Step 1 in any good presentation is to tell them what you're going to tell them. Step 2 is telling them. And Step 3 is tell them what you told them. Repetition is what it's all about—not just droning the same words three times, but finding three different ways of underscoring your major points. This "Rule of 3" is not only reiterative, but it can also address the needs of those with different learning styles (as long as you are creative in the three different ways you serve up the information).

So, in the first part of the class proper, just reveal to the class your class outline (see how helpful those class outlines are?). For example, you might tell a class, "We're going to do some introductory searching of the OPAC, then we're going to take a

> ☞ **Insider Teaching Tip**
>
> Be aware, however, that in this example we've used library jargon (OPAC, service points, stacks) that not everyone in the class may know. When you first use some of this jargon, and no one calls you on it, by all means ask the class: "Does everybody know what an OPAC is?" If anyone in the class looks doubtful, provide the explanation and add, "Hey, you folks are supposed to be keeping me honest about this language thing. Don't let me get away with that again."

short tour of the library and its service points, and finally we're going to go into the stacks so you can actually see how to find a book on the shelf."

As a final note before jumping into the actual teaching, you may want to add, "And please stop me along the way if something is not clear or if you think I've left anything out." We say you MAY want to add this because there might be times when you absolutely have to cover a certain amount of material in a very short time. In such a situation, tell the class, "Please note down and hold your questions for the end and I'll address them then." But always acknowledge that you expect questions from them—it's normal.

TEACHING THEM

How do you teach them? That's the $64,000 question, isn't it? Unlike the $64,000 question, there is no one right or wrong answer to our question, because how you go about teaching them varies enormously depending upon the kind of session you're teaching and to whom you're teaching. We feel comfortable presenting to you a few scenarios of classes and sessions we've taught, and the ways in which we've prepared for them and then taught them. These are examples only, but we think they can serve as models for you to adapt at will.

Teaching Scenario A: The Dog and Pony PR Show

At some point in your career as a librarian, you will most assuredly be involved in a Dog and Pony Show (DPS). No, don't run out and buy a leash and a pair of chaps—the dog and pony show is an unabashed public relations event for the library. The goal of the Dog and Pony Show is to show off the library to its best advantage to those who are not particularly interested in doing any real research at the moment. It may be an open house to generate funding for the library. It may be an orientation session for particular types of users. Or it may be a demonstration of library systems to a board of trustees or a faculty committee.

You may or may not have a good handle on who your audience is going to be in a Dog and Pony Show. So the key to giving a good DPS is to blitz them with what's new and sexy, or whatever services or collections are going to knock their socks off. In a DPS, you're not trying for low-key, you want to "wow" them.

In putting together your class outline for a DPS, concentrate shamelessly on the hottest library stuff you can. Show them the newest Web resources; demonstrate full-text searching and e-mailing of full-image articles; pull out the most beautiful texts; unearth the library treasures. This is not the time to be shy.

If you can identify the target audience, then certainly focus on areas you anticipate are of interest to them. If it's a group of local businessmen, you might want to demonstrate searching LEXIS-NEXIS. If it's the Daughters of the American Revolution, you might want to show them archival materials of local history. If it's the public library trustees, you might want to show them a smorgasbord of resources and services that illustrate how the library is responding to the local community's needs. Keep that audience in mind for every choice you make in what you're going to present.

If your target audience is fairly amorphous or unidentifiable, broaden your presentation. This is where having a good awareness of your library community serves you well. Who might show up at this Dog and Pony Show? Use diverse examples in any searches you do to embrace the variety of potential attendees. Don't confine yourself to a few favorites, show resources and services that will make the library shine.

☛ **Insider Teaching Tip**

A real danger for Dog and Pony Shows is going on for too long. Don't you do it! Stick to Basic Tenet #5: Leave Them Wanting More. A good DPS is short and punchy. It whets their appetites, rather than satiates it. The audience can always come up and talk with you more after a DPS, and chances are you'll want them to. Indeed, the DPS is often just "the start of beautiful friendships."

Teaching Scenario B: The Introduction to the Library OPAC Class

Our goals for introductory OPAC classes are not only to show users how to use the online catalog, but also how to get their hands on the material once they've located it online. So keep this in mind when you see how we prepare such a class.

Heaven only knows which integrated library system your library has (although you notice we are assuming you probably have one). Since everyone reading this will have different systems, we'll give you the brief guidelines for what we cover in our introductions to the OPAC. They include:

a. An explanation of what the OPAC is and what it contains—and what it does not contain. ("The OPAC will give you the listing of journals that the library owns. It will not give you the actual articles themselves.")

☛ **Insider Teaching Tip**

When we started teaching, we usually told students that the OPAC was "an electronic version of the card catalog." We've pretty much stopped doing this because so many of our users have never used a card catalog these days. So be prepared in your classes to give the reverse explanation to today's users: The card catalog was a huge set of index cards in wooden boxes that we used before OPACs were invented.

---

b. An explanation of how to do basic searches. We start with keyword searching since the typical user comes into the library wanting to get material on a topic rather than having a specific author or title of a book. After discussing how to find books using keywords, we segue into author searching (covering compound and non-English names, as well as corporate names for businesses) and then title searching. We often use a journal title as a title search example, since it gives us the opportunity to show students how to look at holdings information to see if we own the specific issue of the journal they need. At some point in this process, we also talk about circulation information and how they can save time by not having to go into the stacks for material that they can see on the computer is checked out.

☛ **Insider Teaching Tip**

Don't use the word SUBJECT in your searching demonstrations except when you really mean it, as applies to subject searching using the Library of Congress Subject Headings. Keyword searching and subject searching can really confuse new and old users alike. In our introductory classes, we sometimes don't even bring up the LCSH: we gauge our audience and see if they either need it or are at the point of being able to use it reasonably well.

---

c. Subject searching: if we think it's appropriate, we will go into subject searching, but usually in a slightly roundabout manner. That is, we teach students how to "finesse" the LCSH; telling them to do a keyword search, identify a book that looks like it's right on the money for their research, and then do a search from the LCSH headings they find for that book. We present this as "power-searching," and tell them that this is the kind of searching they can do "to exploit the system fully." (Power-hungry individuals seem to love this expression; during hands-on practice it's the first thing many entrepreneurial students try or ask about: "Now, how do I exploit the system again?")

☛ Insider Teaching Tip

In every OPAC class we do, we warn students that they may do a search and have the system come back and tell them there are, "Zero results." What should they do then? We tell them to first check for typos in their commands since typing errors account for a good portion of zero result searches. We say they may want to try using different keywords if it's a keyword search. But ultimately we use the ATM analogy with them: if you go to the bank ATM and try to take money out of your account (which you know has money in it) and the ATM tells you the account is empty, do you just walk away from that ATM, accepting their word for it? Not likely! You go to the bank (or call them) and ask, "What gives with my account?" You basically act like an assertive consumer—you know the money's supposed to be in there, and the bank is supposed to make it available to you. So it goes with the library. If the computer tells you there are no books on "environmental racism" in the library, don't just walk away from the computer in disgust. Go to a reference or information desk and ask for help finding material on environmental racism, because more than likely there is information available. This analogy seems to work in just about every situation for a very wide variety of user types.

---

    d. Directions for how to actually find the material on the shelves (which involves brief discussions of the classifications systems, floor plans, holds, recalls, special locations, microforms, e-journals, and current periodical holdings for our libraries).

    e. Information on how to check out material, make photocopies, download bibliographies to disk, or e-mail records to personal accounts.

Teaching Scenario C: The Introduction to the World Wide Web Class

When we teach a World Wide Web introductory class, we have two main objectives: to demonstrate the considerable amount of research students can do on the library's for-pay Web-based resources and to show users how to navigate the Web at large.

    a. The first thing we do in these classes is to poll the group to find out how many are familiar with or have used the Web. Depending on the background information the group gives us in this poll (we may have to define a lot of terms as we go along: cursor, Web browser, Netscape, bookmarks, etc.), we either cover some basic terminology (helped by a basic Web glossary) or dive into the Web itself.

> ### ☞ Insider Teaching Tip
>
> Distribute a basic Web glossary handout in introductory Web classes. We've found such handouts to be a great help to students who are reticent about revealing Web ignorance. It's curious, but we find folks are not so ashamed of library benightedness as they are of not knowing how to use the Web. We make it clear in our classes they have no need of being ashamed of either, but apparently Web illiteracy makes one a social pariah.

b. Then we take the class directly to the library's gateway page, showing them all the links to information about the library, the university, and the Web that they can access there.

> ### ☞ Insider Teaching Tip
>
> To lecture and then go hands-on, or to be interactive live; that is the question. Whether 'tis better to demonstrate a Web resource, have the students watch your demonstration without being online themselves, then have them do hands-on Web navigation when the lecture is done; or to have the students follow your lecture step-by-step at their own keyboards as you do it? Which do we recommend?
>
> For end-user sessions, it's an easy call: lecture first, then hands-on. If the students are working individually at their keyboards, supposedly "following" along with the Web resource you are demonstrating (presumably on a projected screen), they're not paying any attention to what you're saying. They're too busy at their keyboards. You will lose large portions of the class to frozen screens, mouse problems, solitaire, and porn sites. You can fix the glitches and monitor what's on their screens better during a separate, hands-on portion of the class than when you're up in front trying to teach. If you don't have a broadcasting control system that locks the student keyboards and screens, we suggest at least keeping the students' monitors turned off until going to the hands-on portion of the class.

c. From the gateway page we usually go into a "cross-section" of the commercial Web resources to which the library subscribes. In addition to showing how to search these resources, we demonstrate how to print out and download results and e-mail information (including the full-text in some cases) to personal accounts.

☞ Insider Teaching Tip

This is a good point in a presentation to talk about the constant and on-going need to question and evaluate Web information. In talking about the library's gateway page, we emphasize that the resources directly available from that page have been "vetted" by librarians and found to be useful to the library's clientele. We note that once you move a level away from the resources directly connected to the gateway page, the library cannot vouch for where the Web information comes from, or its quality. We have no control over the many links you will encounter throughout the page levels. From here we segue into a broader discussion of navigating the free Web and point out that they always need to question where information comes from: Is it a reliable, unbiased source? A fringe or extremist group? A specific company who's trying to sell you something? A lunatic's garage? All of these are possible Web information providers.

---

d. After demonstrating the "for-pay" databases and resources, we go into some of the freebie, generic sources that may be of interest. We show government sources, pages that help users locate information by subject, other library catalogs (and sites that make it easy to get to them), search engines, and the like. We try to demo a selection of sites that illustrate the good, the bad, and the ugly of what's out there on the Web, and the huge range of what can be found, either advertently or inadvertently. Our focus is on helping users wade through the inconsequential, meretricious, and useless.

Teaching Scenario D: The Course-Related Class

As we talk about subject-specific library classes, we're going to use the terminology that is most familiar to us in an academic setting: a course-related session taught at the specific request of an individual faculty member. The concepts we're talking about here, however, can be applied to any topic-focused library presentation; local history and genealogy presentations come immediately to mind. So please substitute the appropriate words and phrases as they may apply to your particular situation. Club or committee chair, for example, can be overlaid on faculty member. And pardon the fact that our "academic slips are showing"—it's the only way we can write this part fairly fluidly.

For course-related classes, the most important part of preparing for the class is the advance work you do with the faculty member. You can research and prepare yourself into a veritable stupor, but if you haven't gotten enough, or the right, information about what the faculty member hopes are the outcomes from the class, all— or at least much—of your teaching will be for naught. Working at cross-purposes with the faculty member is worse, oftentimes, than doing no class at all.

That said, here are the stages we go through in doing a course-related class:

a. Initial contact with the faculty. You may get a class request in-person, via telephone or voicemail, by e-mail or fax, or on a printed form. We always contact the faculty member (almost always by telephone) and conduct with them what is, in essence, a reference interview for the class prep. To do this, we usually just follow the format of our class request form, which prompts for answers to the questions we have (please see Figure 2–1, Sample Library Instruction Request Form). These questions include: When do they want the class? How many students will be attending? What level are they and how much library knowledge do they have? How long do we have them for? Are there specific skills the faculty member wants instruction in? Or particular resources? Is there a research or writing assignment they will be working on during the term? Can the faculty member give us a copy of her/his syllabus and the assignment, if any? Will the faculty member be attending? (THIS IS KEY! Get them there if at all possible because their presence completely changes the class dynamic. They are sending a message that this is important. Conversely, if they don't attend, they are sending the opposite message.)

☛ Insider Teaching Tip

You can take a step beyond just working from a course syllabus or assignment. Ask the instructor if they have any specific research or paper topics that they know students are working on, and use these for your research examples if you really want to get the class to sit up and pay attention to your searching demonstration.

Figure 2–1: Sample library instruction request form.

Library Instruction Request
Northeastern University Libraries

Return to:

Christine Oka
270 Snell Library
PHONE: (617) 373-3316   TTY: (617) 373-3395   FAX: (617) 373-5409

Northeastern University instructors and faculty may request specialized, course-related library instruction for students by filling out and returning this form to the above address. You may also fax this form; it is helpful if you call and let us know to expect the fax.

We need at least one week's notice to prepare for your class. We will contact you with the final class date, time, and location. **Please note that submitting this form alone does not confirm a session.** For questions or further information, contact Christine Oka, Bibliographic Instruction Coordinator at (617) 373-3316; TTY: (617) 373-3395; or via e-mail: coka@lynx.neu.edu.

Today's date _ _____

Name _____

Campus phone _____ Home phone _____

E-mail address _____

Class/group (dept. & course number or class level: undergrad, graduate) _____

Estimated number of students who will be attending _____

Please give us your preferred dates/times and location for bibliographic instruction

1) _____

2) _____

3) _____

Location: ___ 88 SL (demo classroom) ___ 120 SL (hands-on classroom) ___ Other

We need a description of your students' library research project and which library/ electronic resources to be covered in the instructional session. Use back of sheet if necessary. If there is a syllabus with the written description of the requirements and suggested topic(s) for the research project, please attach a copy to this form.

_____

_____

NOTE: Library Instruction Request forms are now on the World Wide Web. Jump to
http://www.lib.neu.edu/instruct/irf.htm
cko 8/97,7/99r

b. Once our questions have been answered, and we've discussed the goals and overall content of the class with the faculty member, we may suggest additions or changes to the original request based on the length of time available or on new resources of which we are aware that may not have been suggested by the faculty member. The idea of a tour is often a good one to raise, if the faculty member has not suggested it. Alternatively, if the original request is for a tour, and, during the course of discussion, you realize that what the professor really wants is for students to learn to use the online catalog adeptly, you may suggest adding an online demonstration. The main point to keep in mind here, is never assume. Don't assume that the faculty member knows all the resources that might be of use to their students. Do make it clear that this is a collaboration between you and the professor, and that your objective is to enhance their students' library experiences with their help.

☛ Insider Teaching Tip

During the "pre-class interview" with the classroom faculty member, be sure to note that you very much hope they will jump in during the actual class and add their own observations and emphasize any points they really want to get across. Then encourage them to do so also on the day of the class, making it clear to them, and to the students, that you welcome such "interruptions." When the students see you and their regular instructor tossing points back and forth, it acts as a catalyst for learning and discussion.

---

c. Either during, or right after, your initial discussion with the professor, you'll need to schedule the class, book the classroom, make sure the necessary equipment (if any) is available, and possibly recruit a team teacher (combo pairings can be real helpful in this situation. Putting a subject specialist with a teaching or electronic resources expert can be an especially good combination).

d. Once the basic logistics are covered, you'll start preparing for the class. This is where the syllabus and assignment come in so handy: we usually teach directly to the assignment. We typically do some research to get background if it is a subject with which we are not very familiar. This also helps us identify resources we might not at first have considered, as well as helping to provide a context that mirrors the expectations of the group. We almost always create a handout for course-related classes that describes the resources we're presenting and suggests related resources (including related Websites). Use a combination of specific resources and more general ones. Don't forget alternative formats if they apply to the subject or discipline (such as electronic, print, microformat, data, audio-visuals, ephemera, maps, images, gray literature, and slides). At some libraries, librarians actually create Web pages for specific classes. These typically include links to electronic resources to which the library subscribes, as well as links to related information and contact information for help from you, the librarian.

When our information gathering and research are done, and we've sketched out a handout we next prepare the class outline. This mirrors what's on the handout, but acts as our presentation guide. It is especially useful for course-related classes that tend to include a number of segments (for example, electronic demo, instruction in the use of printed products, a tour, and finally hands-on interactive sessions). It may be useful during this process to contact the professor again for more detailed information. Once that class outline is done, we vet it thoroughly to make sure we've got all the elements in there that we need, and then we finalize the handout. After the handout is done, we usually assemble the research packets that we'll distribute at the class (for example, guides to the OPAC, guides to the Web gateway, guides to the library classification system, floor plans and stack locations, library jargon glossaries, and, of course, the specific handout for that class).

☞ Insider Teaching Tip

It's a smart idea to send a draft of the class handout you develop to the faculty member before the library class for review. Ask if this looks like what they wanted and if they have any other suggestions or changes to make. Don't use campus mail for this unless the class is eons in the future: e-mail it!

---

e. It's time to teach the class. It's to be hoped that the professor is there in the classroom with you. If they are, enlist them in the teaching whenever possible. (We have an image of a good class being like a game of toss and catch. This applies to working with faculty as well as with library team teachers. You throw the ball back and forth with somebody always there to catch it.) It's particularly useful if the faculty member reinforces what you're saying; which is more likely if you've done your homework with the faculty member in advance and you are both on "the same page" about what's going to be covered in the class and how. At this point, if you've followed the scenario we suggested above, your work is pretty much done for you. Simply follow the class outline that mirrors the class handout.

Teaching Scenario E: The Multi-session and / or Credit-Bearing Library Class

We mention this scenario mainly because it was the one we first encountered in our library teaching careers. We learned a lot from teaching the credit-bearing classes on which we cut our teeth, but we are aware that many librarians never teach such a class. More importantly for your purposes, you can find huge amounts of information on putting together such classes in the professional educational literature since it more closely follows the kind of teaching done in other classrooms.

We strongly urge you to research the professional educational literature if you will be teaching a multi-session library class. But since there are some differences between other classes and library classes of this type, here are our guidelines and observations about preparing credit-bearing classes and teaching them.

DEVELOPING A COURSE SYLLABUS TO TEACH

Observe the same rule you do for every other class: teach them what they need to know and not more than that. In a multiple-session class, however, you have more room in which to maneuver. You can simply cover more. Sit down and do the "class outline" based on the goals you have for the course, only this time, instead of having to cut down the outline to 1/3rd of its original length, you may actually be able to cover most, if not all, of the points you want to get across.

If you figure that, during the life of the course, you really can cover all that you want to teach, then the next step after developing the overall outline is dividing the course content into manageable, logical single-class sessions. You don't want to try to teach power searching of the OPAC in the same class as teaching in-depth subject searching on the Web. It's covering way too much at one time. So some of the same issues that face you for the one-shot, 50-minute sessions will prevail here. Keep in mind that you can only present a few concepts per class session, and that previewing, teaching, and reiterating them each session takes time.

We developed an assignment for each class in the credit-bearing courses we taught. We structured each class meeting so that we lectured for 20 minutes, then set the students onto doing the assignment. Sometimes assignments were completed in an electronic teaching room, other times they were set in the reference room, and still others took place throughout the library (electronic arcade, special collections, etc.). The assignments changed the pace of the class effectively, as well as the students' interaction with us. We lectured to the entire group collectively, but during the work on the assignment we worked with them in small groups and one-on-one. For some sessions, we brought in colleagues as guest lecturers and team teachers to cover specialized portions of the syllabus so both instructor and student got the benefit of multiple points of view.

TEACHING THAT SYLLABUS

The main difference between these classes and the others we teach is that we wield a certain amount of influence because the course carries credit. You will find that this changes the dynamic of the class, probably in your favor. Students tend to take what you're teaching them more seriously if it is for credit—certainly if it's for a grade—and you may find them listening to you more attentively (or at least seeming to). Since you'll be meeting with the students more than once, you'll have more opportunity to develop a rapport with them. Multi-session courses give you a good opportunity to experiment in your teaching and to learn what's working and what's not. When you get to know a group of students and are working with them over a period of months, they usually give you much more, and better, feedback than you can get in a one-shot class. And they're usually very eager to give you such feedback if they're counting on a grade in a class. You both have vested interests here.

So, too, do you both have more at stake than in a single-session class. You're both investing more into the course: more time, more effort, more of yourselves. So teaching this kind of course can "raise the bar" on your teaching standards. In effect, you will find yourself wanting to make the sessions informative and interesting. And the students will certainly want them so because they're not just closed in that room with you for one 50-minute period, they're in it with you for the long haul. Again, reasons for the class environment to be better overall, but also reasons for putting more demands on your teaching abilities. A credit-bearing class will stretch your personal instructional resources. Be mentally prepared before committing to it.

If you are interested in formally assessing your teaching effectiveness, the multi-session library class is the ideal venue in which to do it since it's feasible to pre-test the students at the beginning of the course, then test them on mid-term exams during the class, and also post-test them for what they learned at the end of the course using a final exam.

Exams were designed to keep our teaching on track throughout the course and long-term as well. The pre-test revealed deficient areas in students' library skills that we would subsequently concentrate on in the first half of the course. At the mid-term, we'd note how many students were and were not "getting it"—if specific sections of the syllabus needed to be re-explained we'd focus on reviewing those parts during the second portion of the course. The final gave us feedback on the overall student absorption of what we'd taught, and helped us revise the course the next time we taught it.

Teaching Scenario F: Staff Training Sessions

The actual teaching of staff training sessions will probably not differ from the teaching you do for end-users. You'll use the same kinds of teaching methods that we've outlined in the previous five scenarios. We would just like to point out, however, that there are some issues about teaching or training staffs that you should acknowledge and of which you should be actively aware before you enter the classroom.

These issues include:

a. The situation can be higher pressure than in teaching end users for a variety of reasons. You'll almost certainly be seeing these folks again and, if yours is a hierarchical organization (which most libraries are), it can be stressful to be in the position of teaching the "higher-ups" in the organization (your boss in particular). We've done it and had very positive experiences, but we were certainly sensitive, before and during the class, to the fact that they were there.

b. You usually get much more sophisticated, in-depth questions from library staff in classes than you do from end-users. This makes sense, since staff members usually know more about the workings of the library than do users and what you're teaching library staff presumably has direct bearing on their daily work lives. We point this out not to make you paranoid, but simply to prepare you for questions that can challenge you more.

c. You will probably not have to explain so much of the library jargon to staff, but keep yourself honest in using specialized terminology and explain it in context the way you would with any group.

d. Staff training tends to be much more frequently hands-on than end-user classes because so much of it tends to be computer-based (demonstrating new library applications, systems, and network features are commonplace kinds of staff training in which you may find yourself involved). You may find it useful to divide such classes into a lecture portion and then a hands-on portion. Or, since staff may already be quite familiar with the basic operations of a system, you may find this a good opportunity to try out a live, interactive class in which the students follow along with you doing hands-on as you demonstrate the applications (not recommended for end-user classes).

e. Make your own calls on how you teach staff. Some people think of it as strictly training. They approach teaching staff in a step-by-step, "rote" manner, showing them how to go from A to B to C in a very specific progression as quickly and as simply as possible. We like to give even more context to what we teach staff than what we're able to present in end-user classes because staff have the background and motivation to go the extra conceptual distance with us, and they may well pass on what we're teaching to other staff and users.

REVIEWING WHAT YOU'VE TAUGHT THEM

When you are gauging the time for any of the six types of classes we've just outlined (the DPS, the OPAC introduction, the Web introduction, the course-related class, the multi-session course, and staff training), allow five to ten minutes at the end of each session in which you reiterate and summarize the major points you covered. To some folks, this sounds like overkill or like a waste of time, but believe us, it isn't. This gives you a last chance to drive your points home.

TELL THEM HOW TO REACH YOU AFTER THE CLASS

Show the attendees in all your presentations your name in print somewhere: on the board, on a business card, or on a handout. Include with it your phone number and e-mail address, or the phone and e-mail for your reference/information desk(s), and/or the URL of your library or departmental Web page. In some cases, you may also want to give them the same contact information for other colleagues in your department, or in other parts of the library, who may be of assistance to them.

THANK THEM FOR COMING

At the end of every class we teach, we open the floor up for questions, asking if the students have had any problems in using the library or if they ran into obstacles getting the materials they want. The final words we utter are usually, "If you don't find what you want, ask for help at a desk. If you need more help than what you get at the desk, call or e-mail me." For electronic demonstrations, we usually emphasize how they can ask for this help remotely via help lines, e-mail, or telephone. This very personal invitation speaks volumes to students who can easily be overwhelmed when they're starting out. For course-related classes, go out of your way to thank the professor for bringing them in to meet with you. They don't have to do it and they are giving up class time to schedule your session. Acknowledge that you are aware of this and express the hope that the professor will bring other classes to you in the future.

It's also just plain good manners to say thank you. And again it shows you to be a regular, decent human being. By the way, if it's been a long class, thank them for their patience. If they were active listeners and asked questions, thank them for being so receptive. But always thank them. Ninety to ninety-five percent of the time they will thank you back, and that's a nice (and rewarding) way to end a class—leaving a good taste in all your mouths.

PHYSICAL PREPARATION OF THE CLASS OUTLINE

Our class outlines vary quite a bit in detail and explicitness, depending upon a number of factors: whether or not we've taught a class before; what the subject matter is; whether it's being team-taught (and therefore needs to be coordinated or "choreographed" between instructors); and what kind of class it is (computer demo, lecture only, lecture and tour, hands-on training, etc.). Since the class outline is something that you alone (or you and only your team teacher) will see, they don't need to look "just so." They can be hastily typed or written outlines. There are two tips we offer about how you make them look.

1. Upsize the typeface to at least 14-16 points so you can read from it easily in the classroom (make it bigger if you're going to be dimming the lights for a computer demo).
2. Put ample spacing between your points so you can read and follow the outline easily in class.

The outline is a point of reference, not the focal point. Your attention should be focused on the students rather than a piece of paper in your hand.

SAMPLE CLASS OUTLINES

In the section that follows you'll find six documents related to class preparation and presentation. Figure 2–2 is an outline for a one-shot class in the humanities for which the instructor requested basic instruction in the use of the library OPAC and subject-related, Web-based resources. Figure 2–3 is the coordinated plan for a class taught by two instructors, showing the division of responsibilities and the choreography between the two. Figure 2–4 is a sample handout that combines a list of resources with basic information about the library. Figure 2–5 is the class plan for the first in a two-part series of classes requested by a history instructor (the first class concentrated on electronic resources, the second on a tour of the reference room and study of printed resources). Figure 2–6 is the handout used with these two library classes. Figure 2–7 is an outline prepared by the instruction program coordinator for use by other instructors in giving one-shot, drop-in introductions to a series of CD-ROM databases.

Figure 2–2: Sample class outline for course-related library class demonstrating OPAC and commercial Web-based library resources.

Class Outline for Humanities Seminar on the American Romantics

Introduction:
Resources and search strategies and using Widener Library

MLA Bibliography
    Note coverage and scope from HOLLIS Plus description.

    Sample search:

        hawthorne and fuller
            Check records 3,4,7,8
            Go to Citation manager and demonstrate how to:
                display them
                e-mail them
                save them

Finding materials in the library: how to look up the following in HOLLIS, the online catalog:

McKinsey, Elizabeth. 1985. Niagara Falls: Icon of the American Sublime. Cambridge: Cambridge UP.

Arrangoiz, Noelle Felice. 1991. "The Representation of Narrative Authority: **Hawthorne**, Cummins, and **Fuller**." *Dissertation Abstracts International*. 52(6):2140A-41A.

Ash, Scott. 1995. "Rereading Antagonism as Sibling Rivalry: The **Hawthorne/Fuller** Dynamic." *American Transcendental Quarterly*. 9(4):313-31.

Go to HOLLIS and get call numbers/locations:

1.   for the McKinsey book: try an author search: au mckinsey elizabeth
     (***don't*** check circulation information for this)

        Widener location listed is: WID-LC F127.N8 M44 1985
        Where will this be in Widener Library?

2.   for the Arrangoiz dissertation: try an author search: au arrangoiz noelle

        Location listed is: at Harvard Depository
        How to get hold of this

3. for the Ash article, do title search for the journal: ti american transcendental quarterly

        Widener location listed is: Philol 707.25
        Ask class: where will this be in Widener?

Doing more searching in HOLLIS:

        Kw cooper and conspiracy
            Do a circulation check / talk about recalls, holds

        Kw whitman and thoreau
            #5
            trace S2
            look at #1
            store all
            send

Talk about HOLLIS Plus more: (just go as far as the scope notes screens of each)

Getting into HOLLIS Plus via subject entry:

        useful files in the humanities subject listing:
            Arts and Humanities Citation index
            Dissertation Abstracts
            JSTOR
            MLA Bibliography
            PCI
            ProQuest Direct

Other resource to mention in Widener Reference Reading Room:

        America: History and Life on CD-ROM

Figure 2–3: Sample class outline "choreographing" a one-shot library class team-taught by a collections' subject specialist and a research services librarian to undergraduates.

Class Outline for Social Sciences Tutorial Library Orientation

The class title is "Producing and Consuming the Good Life: Ideologies of Work and Leisure in East Asia."

Ray welcomes, introduces us, presents an overview of research methods in East Asian studies.

I present HOLLIS and HOLLIS Plus resources: the *Bibliography of Asian Studies*, *PsycInfo*, and *Proquest Direct*.

Student research topics professor provided include:

Tibet and western media.

Taiwan in the new millennium: relation to China, where is it going.

Women's role in Japan today.

Attitudes towards work and leisure in Japan.

Women in the workplace in Vietnam.

How the recent reduction of work hours in many Japanese companies (and also class hours in schools) may be affecting Japanese attitudes toward work and leisure.

Labor and leisure in Vietnam.

Gender ideology and child rearing in Japan.

Japanese women's status/role in society in Japan today . . . feminism, increased number of women in the work force, later age of marriage, the declining birthrate, and how these factors are affecting Japanese society.

Sample search: Japan$ and work and leisure

Ray recaps, concludes, thanks for coming.

Figure 2–4: Sample handout used for a one-shot, course-related library class.

Library Guide for Social Sciences E-100 Proseminar
Instruments of Statecraft

A VERY Quick Introduction to Research in Widener Library

To help guide you successfully through Widener, there are a number of library materials in this packet, including:

a map of the campus with libraries highlighted;

Widener Library's hours of operation;

HOLLIS and HOLLIS Plus guides (the former tells you just about everything you'll need to know about searching HOLLIS [the Harvard University online library catalog]; the latter tells you how to get to HOLLIS Plus [Harvard University Library's World Wide Web information navigator]); and two essential pieces of paper for doing research in Widener: a two-sided, two-color (black and crimson) sheet that shows classification numbers and their floor/wing locations, and a plan of the Widener stacks.

There are ten levels of book stacks in Widener: you'll enter on Level 1 near the Circulation Desk on the 1st Floor. The stacks go up six levels from Level 1, and down four levels (from A to D). On D Level there is a tunnel that leads to an additional, connected three levels of stack: Pusey Library Levels P1-P3.

There are HOLLIS and HOLLIS Plus terminals on the second floor of Widener, near the Information Desk and the Reference Desk in the Loker Reading Room. Search HOLLIS Plus to locate journal articles, essays, government documents, and books on the topic, individual, or organization you are researching. Then use HOLLIS to get the call numbers and locations of books and journals in Widener Library.

About HOLLIS Plus Resources
The following HOLLIS Plus files may be of particular use to you in doing research for this proseminar. To use them, go to the main *HOLLIS Plus* screen and under, "All other resources," click on the "Listed alphabetically" section. Please note: anyone can access HOLLIS Plus remotely by pointing their Web browser at: *http:// hplus.harvard.edu*. Some HOLLIS Plus files can be used by any and all users remotely. However, many of the files listed below require a valid Harvard ID for remote access; for these files you will be asked for a Harvard ID and name when accessing them from a location outside the library.

Figure 2–4 *Continued*

Figure 2–4 Continued

AccessUN: provides online access to the Readex United Nations Index of current and retrospective United Nations documents and publications. Documents from the six main bodies of the United Nations (General Assembly, Security Council, Economic and Social Council, Trusteeship Council, Secretariat, and International Court of Justice) are indexed. Full-text resolutions from the General Assembly, Security Council, and the Economic and Social Council are appended to their respective bibliographic citations. The file currently contains citations to documents from 1961 to the present. Full texts of selected documents are available, including resolutions from the General Assembly beginning with 1981, the Security Council beginning with 1974, and the Economic and Social Council beginning with 1982. Selected provisional verbatim and summary records of the General Assembly and Security Council beginning with 1990 are included.

Columbia International Affairs Online (CIAO): a comprehensive source for theory and research in international affairs. It publishes a wide range of scholarship, from 1991 on, that includes working papers from university research institutes, occasional papers' series from non-governmental organizations, foundation-funded research projects, and proceedings from conferences. It has more than 160 links to international affairs centers, institutes, and resources; U.S., international, and foreign government sites; environmental studies Web pages; and news media services.

Congressional Universe: produced by Congressional Information Service, this contains many full-text resources such as the Congressional Record, hearings testimony, bills, etc., and other indexing services such as indexes to National Journal and Congress Daily. It connects the user to indexes, abstracts, and full text of primary documents of national public policy and legislation. Its indexes and abstracts go back to 1970. Other parts of the database cover various time periods.

PAIS International: indexes public policy literature, with emphasis on contemporary issues and the making and evaluating of public policy. Worldwide in scope, PAIS indexes publications from 1972 on in English, French, German, Italian, Portuguese, and Spanish.

PolicyFile: provides convenient, efficient, online access to public policy research and analysis from think tanks, university research programs, research organizations, and publishers from 1990 on.

ProQuest Research Library: indexes about 2,000 journals in all academic fields. Full text is available for about one half of the journals included and is searchable.

Full images are available from 1988 on, full text from 1992 on, and text plus graphics is available from 1995 on.

United Nations and Other International Organizations: is an alphabetically-arranged set of links to almost every Internet-accessible United Nations Web and Gopher site as well as links to other international organizations.

You may also find it useful to:

1. Look at *KSG OPIN, the Kennedy School Online Political Information Network* on the Web, at: *http://www.ksg.harvard.edu/~ksgpress/opin/index.html.*

2. Browse the Governmental Resources and Social Sciences subject sections of HOLLIS Plus for more relevant indexes and research tools (at the main HOLLIS Plus screen, under "All other resources," click on "Listed by subject" to access these sections).

3. Go to the Government Documents and Microforms Service Desk in Lamont Library (first floor) for assistance with research in this area.

A Last Word to Save Your Valuable Time:
Widener Library is a huge, incredibly rich research resource. It can take a little time and effort to learn your way around it, but you will find materials here that are available, individually or collectively, in very few other places in the world. If you don't find what you're looking for, or if you need some help focusing on what to look for, please do go to the Reference Desk in the Loker Reading Room and ask for assistance. The Reference Librarians there can save you lots of time and many steps as you work in Widener.

My office phone number is 617-496-4226. If you have e-mail and would like to address a question to me, my e-mail address is: *claguard@fas.harvard.edu.* Good luck with your research.

Cheryl LaGuardia

Figure 2–5: Sample class plan for the first in a two-part library class series (the first class devoted to online resources, the second to print resources and a tour) for a graduate seminar.

Please note that Figure 2–6, which follows, is the library handout that was prepared and distributed to the students for use in the two classes.

Roosevelt seminar class plan
C. LaGuardia

Before class: Bookmark the ABC-CLIO and citing sites

Introduction:
Pragmatic A-Z approach to starting up research in Widener Library

1. HOLLIS searching

   Au samuels, peggy
   Ti don't you dare shoot that bear
   Kw theodore roosevelt biography
   HD, circulation and holdings information, store, and send

2. HOLLIS Plus searching:
   a. show how to get to OED and Encyclopedia Britannica: OED: search quotations: roosevelt and stick; EB: theodore roosevelt
   b. America: History and Life: gender roles and theodore roosevelt output options, full display, e-mail
   c. point out Archives USA
   d. History Online: talk about, don't go into
   e. JSTOR—do quick search on theodore roosevelt in history journals
   f. Periodicals Contents index: select American history and do search on Theodore Roosevelt and women
   g. talk about getting in by subject: humanities and social sciences

3. mention the print resources that we'll look at during the Widener tour in two weeks

4. citing electronic resources—show site

Figure 2–6: The library handout that was used for the class described in the previous outline.

Brief Library Guide for
SSCI E-100 Introduction to Graduate Study in Social Sciences
Spring Term 1999 Graduate Proseminar, History and Government
Wednesday, March 3, 1999, 6:15 PM, ELF 1, Lamont Library

Suggestions for Starting Your Research in Widener

1. Consult reference books in the reading room
   Check reference books in the Loker Reading Room (2nd floor of Widener) to get an overview of your topic. A few suggested biographical tools and chronologies to use include:

   American National Biography. Widener Reading Room: RR 1711.20

   Dictionary of American Biography. Widener Reading Room: RR 1711.2

   Encyclopedia of American Facts and Dates. Widener Reading Room: RR 3637.6

   Encyclopedia of American History. Widener Reading Room: RR 3627.10.6

   National Cyclopedia of American Biography. Widener Reading Room: RR 1711.8

   Notable American Women. Widener Reading Room: Widener: RR 1711. 34

   Theodore Roosevelt, 1858–1919; Chronology, Documents, Bibliographical aids. Widener: Roosevelt Collection (4 West) 100.B56

2. Search HOLLIS, the online catalog
   Search *HOLLIS* for books at Harvard on specific subjects/individuals, as well as to get call numbers for journals at Harvard:

   HOLLIS Searches (consult the *HOLLIS Reference Guide* in your packet for more searching details):

   > Use a keyword (kw) search if you are "fishing" for information:
   > kw roosevelt spanish american war

   > Use an author search if you have a book author's name:
   > au burnham, john

   > Use a title (ti) search if you have the title of a journal and need to locate it on the shelf to get at a specific article. When searching for journal titles, it may be helpful to "limit" your search to "serials only," thusly:
   > ti journal of american history//fo=ser

Figure 2–6 *Continued*

Figure 2–6 *Continued*

Once you have the Widener call number (or "class number"), check the double-sided *Widener Library Location Chart* (crimson on one side, black on the other) to locate the stack level and wing in which you'll find the book. Enter the stacks on the 1st floor of Widener, near the Circulation Desk.

3. Search HOLLIS Plus resources for articles, book chapters, etc.

    a. There are some helpful general purpose resources on HOLLIS Plus. Under Resources listed by Subject there's a category, Dictionaries and Encyclopedias, in which you'll find, for example, both the *Oxford English Dictionary, 2nd Edition*, and the *Encyclopedia Britannica Online*. Both are useful for getting background information, to check terminology, names, dates, and to locate related sources. (Be on the lookout for very up-to-date Internet links on *Britannica*.)

    b. Specific HOLLIS Plus databases of use to you for this class include:

        America: History and Life (at a HOLLIS Plus terminal, set the browser to: *http://serials.abc-clio.com/*). *America: History and Life* is a bibliographic index of the history of the United States and Canada from prehistory to the present. Published since 1964, the database covers over 2,000 journals published worldwide. Over 90% of the articles included are published in English-language journals.

        Archives USA: contains information about manuscript and archival collections from the National Union Catalog of Manuscript Collections (NUCMC) and the National Inventory of Documentary Sources (NIDS). It also updates and supersedes the Directory of Archives and Manuscript Repositories in the United States (DAMRUS) last published in 1988.

        History Online: provides online indexing to the *Times of London* and the *New York Times* as follows: the file includes *Palmer's Index to the Times* (of London), *1790–1905*; the *Official Index to the Times* (of London) (the current release contains data from the years 1906 to 1920 and 1970 to 1980); and the *Historical Index to The New York Times* (whose current release contains data from the years 1863 to 1879).

Note Well: There is a longer period of indexing to *The NY Times* available in the printed *New York Times Index* in the Reading Room (see below).

        JSTOR: consists of over 70 journal titles in varied topics (from ethnology to economics) and contains actual journal page images. *JSTOR* allows browsing and full text searching of the journals.

        Periodicals Contents Index (PCI): an index to the contents of thousands of journals in the humanities and social sciences, from their first issues into the 1990s. It covers journals from North America, the United Kingdom, and the rest of the English-speaking world, and journals in other European languages including French, German, Italian, and Spanish. *PCI* includes the complete table of contents for each issue of each journal. Bibliographic records are also included for the journals themselves and every journal is indexed under one or more of 37 subject headings, e.g.: economics, history, law, literature, political science, and religion.

c. to find other subject-specialized resources on HOLLIS Plus:

Go into the "All other resources" section of *HOLLIS Plus*. If you don't know a specific index you want to search, click on "Listed by subject" and browse the Social Sciences and Humanities sections.

4. Use print resources in the Widener Reading Room
   A few of these include:

The American Historical Association's Guide to Historical Literature (located in Grossman: Ref Z6201.A55 1995 and in the Widener Reading Room: RR 3601.2). Section 43, *United States, 1877-1920* (Vol. 2, pages 1412+) provides an extensive bibliography of materials that may be of particular use to you in this course.

The New York Times Index (the printed index to *The New York Times*): RR 683.15

Poole's Index to Periodical Literature (an index to nineteenth-century magazines): RR 663.5

Reader's Guide to Periodical Literature (an index to twentieth-century magazines): RR 663.1

Go to the Reference Desk in Widener's Reading Room for help both in identifying and finding materials if you have any difficulty. The reference librarians know the collections well and can suggest other tools for you to use throughout the library.

For Your Bibliographies
If you'd like some help for Web-based resources in your bibliography, you may find the following Website useful:

http://www.niagara.edu/library/turabian.html

(You can find a larger listing of sites for citing electronic research resources by going into Alta Vista on HOLLIS Plus and doing the search, "citing electronic resources"; the example given is just one sample).

If you would like to schedule an individual research consultation with a Research and Bibliographic Services Librarian, please call Jan Weiner at 495-2971.

Figure 2–7: Sample class outline done by an instructional coordinator to distribute to other instructors for use in drop-in workshops.

For Noon Workshop Instructors: thanks for agreeing to teach in the noon workshop series. Here's the instructor outline for teaching the Monday Noon Workshops. We want to keep this simple to give students a basic orientation to these databases. Just so you know, an updated CD-ROM handout is in the works and will be ready to use for these workshops.

NOON WORKSHOP OUTLINE

√ WELCOME to the Library: include your name and the fact that you work at the Reference Desk and teach classes on doing research in the library and using electronic resources.

√ List the databases you will be showing them.

√ Mention the new, upgraded workstations in the Reference Area and that, in the future, we hope to have campuswide access to these resources.

√ Mention that most of these databases use Windows and a mouse to maneuver through the system. It helps to mention the trackball mouse option on the Reference Area workstations (so they aren't thrown when they go up to use those workstations).

√ Describe the database (you can use the information off the CD-ROM handout) and then show them:

➡ how to "get in" to the database(s)

➡ how to search

➡ how to navigate the system

➡ display options (all fields, full screen, etc.)

➡ how to print

➡ how to download (explaining WHY they'd want to do that; i.e., save trees, it works if the printer is out of paper (or out of order), and it makes it easier to put together a bibliography when used in tandem with their word processing software program.

√ If it's a bibliographic database, *briefly* explain that they will have to check the NU Libraries catalog in order to know a) if the library owns the material being cited, and b) where it's located in the library.

√ Conclusion: summarize (tell 'em what you've told them) and *thank them for coming.*

REFERENCES

1. Vernon A. Magnesen. 1983. "A Review of Findings from Learning and Memory Retention Studies." *Innovation Abstracts* 25 (September 16): 3–4.
2. Tori Coward. 1993. "How Users Learn is Vital to How You Should Train." (Part 2). *Infoworld* 15 (April 12): 58 (1).

Chapter 3

LESS INTERACTION, MORE STRUCTURE

*If you would not be forgotten, as soon as you are dead
and rotten, either write things worth reading, or do
things worth the writing.*
Benjamin Franklin, *Poor Richard's Almanac*

There are circumstances, usually in speaking situations rather than classes, when the occasion calls for less spontaneous presentation interaction and more ahead-of-time preparation and structure on your part. You probably have a set number of minutes to make your case and then sit down or mingle with the attendees. These occasions include high-profile Dog and Pony Shows for VIPs, speeches on behalf of the library to the public, or professional conference talks. Under these circumstances, we often do canned computer demonstrations using presentation software or work from a script (both give you greater control over the length of your talk, allowing you to time how long you'll be "on").

PRESENTATION SOFTWARE

We use Microsoft PowerPoint for our computer presentations, but there are a number of software packages like it out there that will accomplish the same end product: combine text and graphics to give "canned" demonstrations. Frankly, we love PowerPoint because it's easy to learn and use. Our first experience with it came under quite a bit of pressure: The day before an important demonstration to some visiting dignitaries, we were told that the library's systemwide network was going to be taken down the day of the presentation. We had approximately 18 hours from hearing this to the hour when the presentation was to be delivered. Fortunately, somebody in our computer support department had an extra copy of PowerPoint on hand and gave it to us. We installed the software and sat down at the keyboard that afternoon. By the evening we had put together a pretty decent, working presentation. It was sufficiently seamless that most of the people at the demo didn't realize we weren't doing a live presentation.

While we don't recommend learning how to use presentation software under these circumstances, we take every opportunity we can to sing PowerPoint's praises for saving our bacon that day.

So, having established ourselves as enthusiastic proponents of the appropriate use of presentation software, we must now implore you not to use it as a "script crutch." The idea of using presentation software is to make good use of the computer offline to get your presentation points across, incorporating graphics (including screen captures), sound, color, and movement. The idea is not to put the entire presentation, word for word, on the screen and just read from it.

And yet, we're aghast at the number of speakers we've seen use PowerPoint or other presentation software in just this way at conferences and workshops. It's not very different from having overhead transparencies with the speech written out on them, and the speaker reading from each sheet (the only appreciable difference being that transparencies are easier for the conference organizers to arrange, since they're technologically a notch less challenging than a computer demo). But the effect on the audience is exactly the same . . . ZZZZZZZ.

Here are our ideas for using presentation software, modestly entitled:

THE SEVEN COMMANDMENTS OF THE CANNED DEMO

1. Thou shalt design the canned demo in high contrast colors and a large type font, remembering that many of the templates the system provides may look peachy-keen on a small computer screen, but they will fade and blur when magnified and projected on a 10-foot by 20-foot wall screen and that 12-point type will not be readable beyond the first row of seats.

2. Thou shalt start the presentation with an initial screen that giveth the title of thy talk, thy name (and affiliation if thou're not giving the presentation on thine home turf), the date, and the occasion (conference title, etc.).

3. Thou shalt do the presentation in outline form (and never, ever, read word for word off the screen). Include thine major points only, and plan to extemporize or fill in the details as thou proceeds.

4. Thou shalt not crowd the screens with too many points. Put no more than four or five ideas on each screen.

5. Thou shalt use the system's bells and whistles wisely. (Desisting from making the thing look like a silent movie or MTV video unless that's really the image

thou wants to convey. Special effects can overwhelm the content of thine presentation very quickly and detract from the overall impact.)

6. Thou shalt honor Basic Tenet #5! (Leave Them Wanting More, Not Less.)
7. Thou shalt finish with an "End" or "Finish" screen, signifying to thy audience that thou art done.

We've supplied a sample PowerPoint presentation in Figure 3–1 to show how these commandments should be incorporated into a canned demo.

Figure 3–1: Sample PowerPoint presentation.

A Rocky Romance
with Electronic Classrooms

By Cheryl LaGuardia
Coordinator of the
Electronic Teaching
Center
Harvard College Library
NEBIC / June 12, 1998

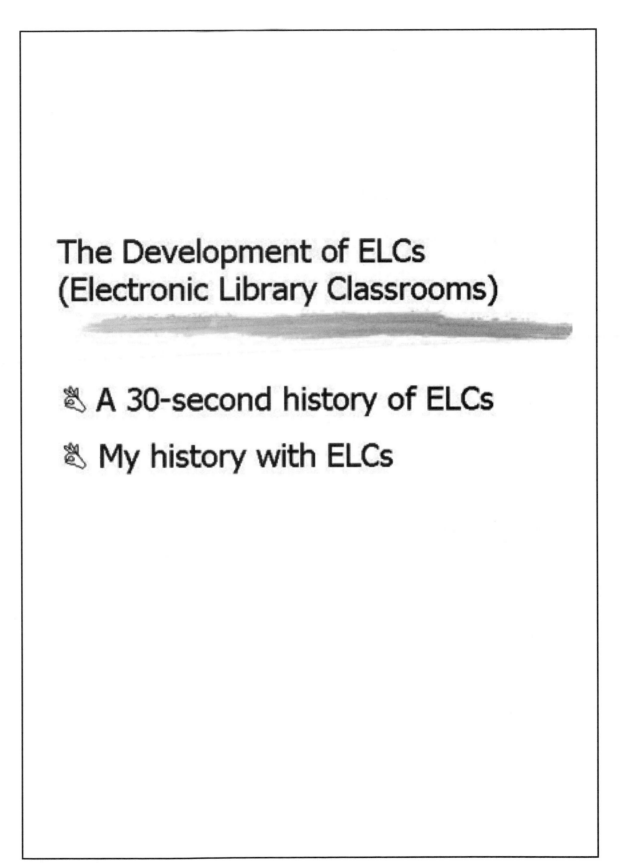

The Classroom Love/Hate Quiz

① Why?

② Who?

③ When?

④ Where?

⑤ What?

⑥ How?

Make It Simple (Pre-Answer the Often Overlooked Questions)

- Redundancy features
- Screen: right kind? Works easily?
- Seating: extra needed? Stacking?
- Space: ADA, roving, people size

finis

PREPARING AND USING SCRIPTS

When we use the term, "script," we generally mean a word-for-word manuscript from which you'll read a presentation. The only exception to this meaning that we can think of applies to scripts that we've developed as instructional coordinators: suggesting the points for others to follow in a set of similar, multiple-class sessions. In this latter case, the script we developed was really a suggested outline rather than a word-for-word version of what to say (to see an example of one of these, go back and look at Figure 2–7 among the sample outlines in the previous chapter). So, here we'd like to talk a bit about preparing the word-for-word type of script.

As we said earlier in this book, we think there's a time and a place for using scripts, and that's for high-profile, anxiety-producing public presentations to large crowds of people you're unlikely to know or to see again. Scripts do not work well in library classes, usually because they defeat the back-and-forth, question-and-answer dynamic that is the best and most effective part of a live class. But if you're involved in library instruction, there's a very good chance that you will be called on to do some kind of Dog and Pony Show or professional conference presentation at some point in your career (we hope you'll even seek these opportunities out once you've finished reading this book and gotten some teaching under your belt).

For those occasions when it is appropriate to use a script, here's the means we use to prepare it and how we deliver the speech:

---

1. Write it

2. Prepare the manuscript for reading

3. Read it

We're a little worried that this very simple looking list may make scripts look overly appealing to new teachers. So let's go into the details of what this list involves.

WRITE IT

Write the script out like an essay: a beginning, a body, and a conclusion. But remember to put EVERYTHING you're going to say in there (thanks for letting me speak to you today, thanks for coming, thanks for listening to me). A good speech needs to read like both a well-thought out article and a good conversation. Remember it's being spoken, so you want to use words that sound well together on the air rather than just persuasive language that will lie well on the page. (Are you starting to get the idea that this is not as simple as it first sounded? Good.)

PREPARE THE MANUSCRIPT FOR READING.

Well, that's simple enough, isn't it? Ya print it out, right?

Yes, you do print it out, but you print it out in a particular way. First off, you're reading this. In most situations where you're reading from a script, you will have minimal control over the lighting in the room. You may be co-presenting with someone who's using an overhead projector and they, therefore, may need to keep the lights lower in intensity than normal. If you wear glasses, glare from too much light can be a problem when trying to read from a script.

To avoid these problems, and to make it as easy as possible to read the words off the page, upsize your print font size to at least 18 points (depending upon your eyesight; we sometimes go as high as 24-point type if there's a chance the room is going to be quite dark).

Increasing point size of type has two advantages: it makes the print easy to read, plus it reduces the amount of information you put on each page of the script. Confine yourself to one or two sentences per page—no more—and "parse" the script into many pages. Why? Because this will help pace your talk. New or nervous speakers tend to speak incredibly fast. If you have to flip a page for each thought or sentence, you will slow down out of necessity. Remember that you are probably talking a lot faster than you realize when you present. Three seconds seems like an eon during a speech, but going slower and speaking more distinctly makes you sound and look better as a speaker.

Another trick about preparing the manuscript that a canny colleague (who is a superb, well-prepared public speaker) shared with us years ago is to carry your script to the presentation site in a box like the kind good stationery comes in. If you've followed our advice about font and pagination, you're going to have a honking big pile of paper (for any speech longer than 5 minutes). Keeping it in the box keeps it organized. (AND DON'T FORGET TO INSERT PAGE NUMBERS! ALWAYS!!!!) It also gives you something to keep the speech in just in case the speaking site lacks an adequate presentation surface. Most podia are slanted: do you want your entire script to slide off the podium onto your ankles just as you get up to speak? Probably not. Get the box.

READ IT

Well for heaven's sake, just how simple-minded can we be? Right? Of course you'll read the speech, that's the whole point!

But when we say "read it," we really mean:

a. Read it to yourself when you've finished writing it.
b. Then read it aloud to yourself.
c. Then read it aloud to yourself inserting pauses, changes in voice tone and volume, and adding appropriate gestures and facial expressions (the theatrics, if you will).

d. Then read it aloud to a friend (using the pauses, changes in voice, etc.).

e. Then read it aloud to another friend (if you have two, really patient, long-suffering friends who listen actively and well).

f. Make any changes that need to be made (listen to your friends' feedback—they can tip you off to whether or not you're droning or, alternatively, going over the top).

g. Now you're ready to read the speech to your audience.

As far as content is concerned, the one piece of advice we offer for preparing the content of a speech is to use the same information gathering techniques about your audience that you use for a class. Whenever possible, know to whom you are speaking and what they are looking for. You should be able to get this information from the person who asks you to speak or present, whether this is at a local get-together or rally or at a national convention. If they don't offer you a "characterization" of your audience, be sure you ask for it.

We don't want to tell you the number of times we have attended conferences and had non-librarian speakers make an address obviously not having targeted at the group who shows up. Whether this is because they didn't bother to find out who their audience was going to be, or because they are recycling a canned speech they have used umpteen times before, we don't know. But please, don't YOU do this. About recycling speeches: do it at your peril. If you always deliver exactly the same message, why should anyone bother to come hear you speak? At least serve it up a little differently each time.

Chapter 4

CLASSROOM DYNAMICS: HANDLING THE CLASS

I was gratified to be able to answer promptly, and I did.
I said I didn't know.

Mark Twain, *Life on the Mississippi*

What we're really talking about here is controlling the class: keeping the students' focused; keeping the class on target and going at the right pace; and dealing with hecklers, noisy students, or the uninterested. This may or may not be a big issue for you in your teaching, but we figure it can't hurt at least to go over a few of the premises and techniques about being "masters of your own domains."

We start a class or presentation by getting everyone's attention. Before the class starts, we arrange our outlines and make sure the equipment is ready to go. When it's time to begin, we stand "front and center" in the classroom, face the class, and tell them it's time to start. We wait for any talking to stop.

DEALING WITH DISRUPTERS

And what do you do if it doesn't stop? There are a number of devices we routinely use to get students' attention (or regain it) and deal with the potentially disruptive or unruly.

When you've announced that you're ready to start the class, if talking doesn't stop immediately, wait a few seconds, looking around the room. Look pointedly, and inquiringly, at whomever may still be talking, as if to say, "Do you have something important that we all need to hear?" Direct your, and the rest of the class's attention, at whomever is keeping you from beginning. That usually stops unintentional conversational stragglers.

Some students just can't seem to stop talking in a class. A pair of students may try to converse throughout your lecture. One effective way of dealing with this is to stop the class dead, look at them, and wait for them to realize their voices are the only ones in the room. Or, you can try very obviously to talk over them (which can strain your vocal cords; not recommended). Instead, we intentionally talk more softly, so that, again, their voices are the only ones that can be heard in the room. Both tactics may, indeed, embarrass rude individuals, but note that *you are not doing anything actively to embarrass them, they have embarrassed themselves. This is important.* Treat students with respect at all times. In these instances, they will find themselves, in effect, stopping the class and coming under the other students' censure. This effect often stops the magpies.

In general we suggest that you not single out any student with negative attention unless they are so disruptive you can neither ignore their behavior nor proceed effectively with the class. If, however, a student continually interrupts you during the lecture, either to make tangential points or to ask disruptive questions, try this: turn and face them, make direct eye contact with them, and say that the point is something you would very much like to go into in detail with them after the class, but that for now the class needs to move forward. Speak slowly, firmly, and distinctly for emphasis.

Whatever else you do, don't lose your cool during the class. Employ the previous tactic asking them to talk with you after class once, then stop engaging with any student who's baiting or "over-questioning" you. If necessary, make eye contact, smile, and repeat gently, but firmly, "after class."

If none of these methods work to keep a student from disrupting the class, we suggest you stop the class and ask the student to step outside the classroom so you can speak with them. When you meet them outside, explain that you have a class to teach to a whole roomful of other students and that you will meet with them when the class is done to address any special questions they may have. Do not confront a student in the classroom because you're liable to lose the class's pace, control, and respect. Step outside the classroom to speak with the resistant solo disrupter. (Please note that in our combined years of teaching this has happened on average less than once a year. So don't expect it to be the norm. It is definitely "exceptional" behavior.)

LOSING THEM, GETTING THEM BACK, AND KEEPING THEM

If you think you're losing the class's attention, or if you think you've gotten them so confused they don't know what you're doing anymore, stop and ask the class at large, "Is this not making sense?", "Have I lost you folks?", or "Am I in Paris and are you somewhere on the Great Plains?" (if you like to use metaphor…). This doesn't demean either you or them, but it refocuses your teaching and their attention.

You'll notice that making eye contact has suddenly become the norm for managing the class. Our initial strategy for making "fake" eye contact with the forehead is recommended only for the early stages of your presentation, when you may be unnerved or distracted by interacting directly with the class. The reality of teaching, however, is that if you really want to connect with the class, to engage them in the learning process, you have to personalize the situation and deal with them as human beings. You need to read the feedback they are giving you with their expressions and eyes. So, as you become an adept teacher, you will learn to do "spot checks" on whether or not they're "getting it" by reading their countenances.

The ultimate rule of thumb about keeping their attention, and respect, is this: don't be afraid to say you don't know something. You can phrase your "I don't know" answer in different ways: "That's a good question—nobody's ever asked me that before. Let me find out" or "I don't know the answer to that. Let's see if we can find out." (We use this one in online situations when we think looking for the answer will, in itself, be instructive.) Sometimes just, "I don't know, but I'll find out and get back to you" works very well. Whenever you say you'll follow up, by the way, make sure you do so or you'll ruin whatever carefully constructed credibility you established during the class.

You don't have to be apologetic about not knowing something. Frankly, it can make some students feel much more of a connection with you and your teaching to hear you say you don't know something. Anyone who represents that they know it all is inhuman—and not a good teacher.

Chapter 5

CONSTANT RENEWAL: LEARNING FROM YOUR TEACHING

*Do not seek to follow in the footsteps of the men of old;
seek what they sought.*

Basho, *The Rustic Gate*

To round off this discussion of learning to teach in libraries, we'd like to talk about how, having learned to teach, you can maintain your interest in instruction long-term. Not to put a damper on anyone's enthusiasm, but this is most definitely an issue for library teachers. How do you keep it fresh? How do you stay jazzed about teaching after doing 25 carbon-copy "Introduction to the OPAC" classes in a month? How do you keep a positive attitude when you're walking into your fourth class of the day? Although not talked about nearly as much as "reference burnout," library instruction burnout is a very real problem that needs to be addressed.

To maintain your effectiveness, you need to revisit a number of the same issues that were covered in the first part of this book: the physical, mental, and organizational preparation that you're using to teach. To these you may need to keep in mind yet another, crucial consideration: don't teach too much. Although it may not seem possible to do so at this point in your instructional career, believe us. It is a very real possibility that there will be days when you are teaching way too much. Why? Mostly because success breeds more success. As you improve as a teacher, you will want to do it more. It grows on you. And word will get around that you give a bang-up good class (word of mouth is your best advertiser for library instruction) and others will want to make use of your services. Since business may have been slow when you

---

SIDEBAR

BI-L

BI-L is the library instruction Internet discussion listserv maintained by Martin Raish at Brigham Young University. We highly recommend it to all instructors, new and experienced. It is a wonderfully rich resource of shared information. The members of this list are particularly generous in sharing their time and knowledge. To subscribe to the list, send the following message to listserv@byu.edu: sub bi-l yourfirstname yourlastname

---

started out, you take on more and more classes—you never say no. The number of classes snowballs quickly.

The first thing you have to learn to do as the instructional snowball starts rolling down the hill is to say, "No," before it becomes an avalanche and buries you. Pace yourself. Go back over the physical preparation list in Part 1 and see if you're sticking to it. Are you getting enough sleep? Are you allowing yourself enough time to get from one class to another, or are you so tightly scheduled you don't have time even to eat lunch? Are you finding yourself up in front of a class with a bladder so full (since there was no time to make it to the restroom between classes) you're afraid of spontaneous explosion?

Take heed of these danger signals. You are fast approaching burnout. You can keep up this kind of behavior for only a very short period of time before it affects your life negatively—in major ways—if you don't achieve some balance.

Learn what your limits are and set them. If you drag home and can barely eat dinner after doing three classes in a day, set your per day class limit at two and see if your energy level comes back. Try new teaching strategies, or rediscover some that worked well for you in the past. If you feel enervated from doing classes by yourself, enlist a colleague to team teach with you and see if the interaction between you revives your instructional interest.

It pays to reinvest in your teaching periodically. What do we mean by reinvest? Attend library instructional conferences, sign up on BI-L (please see BI-L sidebar) and join in the electronic conversations there, read more in the professional literature about instructional techniques, or try out some new classes yourself and then write something for the professional library literature about it. Participate in teaching workshops, organize informal discussions with your colleagues about teaching, and take the class in public speaking at the local adult education center if you haven't already.

No matter how accomplished a teacher you are, you can always learn something new, something different, and something effective, from watching others and talking to them about instruction. After you've taught in a particular way for awhile, it may be a good idea to do some new role-playing. Try on some new persona in your next class and see how it fits. When you feel like you're in a teaching rut, undertake to teach an entirely new class. It will require you to concentrate and re-channel your mind and energies.

Sometimes, when we're feeling a little teaching-jaded, we like to read the writings of those with whose opinions we thoroughly disagree. It gets our instructional blood up, so to speak, and reminds us that we have strong beliefs about what we do and are committed to doing excellent work. A wide diversity of opinion about instructional methods is inevitable, given the variety of teaching and learning styles that exist. And thank heaven for it! There is nothing so invigorating as setting out to challenge the status quo or the opinion of another.

We need to stress just how much team teaching can help keep your interest and effectiveness as an instructor alive. The physical, emotional, and logistical support it provides is invaluable to the long-term library teacher. Post-class debriefing sessions are a great boost if you're feeling weary and over used. They give you a chance to talk about specific issues of interest to you as a teacher, they afford the opportunity to resuscitate your own feedback-giving skills, and they give you a legitimate—yet safe—opportunity to talk about how you're doing with classes. Good debriefing sessions from team-taught classes are ongoing positive touchstones of a dynamic instructional program. And let's face it, team teaching gives you the never-ending opportunity to learn new and good instructional techniques from peers you respect.

MAKE IT YOUR OWN

We've presented to you a number of techniques that have worked to revitalize and, in some cases, reinvent our teaching. We've emphasized how much you can learn from others, how you should role play, and borrow the smart methods from others. But a word here near the end about making your teaching your own.

It is, admittedly, easier, faster, and sometimes highly effective to learn from others—to borrow from them and to build on what you learn from them. But we'd like to urge you ultimately to learn to trust your own teaching instincts and to be guided by them. You will certainly find many instances when the work of others is of great use to you in trying out new methods, or just in getting through a difficult class. But be open and receptive to the spontaneous moments that will come in your teaching; the times when everything gels and you synthesize an entirely new approach to a class or demonstration. This happens more frequently than you might think, so long as you preserve your receptivity to students and remain flexible in the actual teaching of the class. There are instructional epiphanies to be had—we've experienced them—and they add enormously to the class in which they occur, as well as to the core of your permanent teaching knowledge. Look for them and take advantage of them when they come. You may invent a NEW teaching wheel in the process.

Conclusion

WHAT EVERY SUCCESSFUL TEACHER KNOWS

How you gonna keep 'em down on the farm, now that they've seen Paree?
Lewis and Young, *Song title and lyric, 1919*

We've tried in this book to pass along the techniques, skills, and knowledge that we've learned from teaching in libraries for . . . more years than we care to admit to. But you may have noticed that, except for talking about burnout and a few slightly "touchy-feely" passages here and there, we haven't really discussed how we feel about teaching. This is simply because you won't believe us if we describe teaching's emotional rewards. You've got to learn about them firsthand (remember that Tertullian quote in the Preface about persuading versus teaching?).

We're not going to try to persuade you that, if you take the time to learn how to teach and aim at teaching well, it will be enormously satisfying. We're pragmatists and we figure you're reading this book either because you want to (in which case we don't have to convince you) or because you feel you must (in which case we're not going to "convince" you of anything). The proof will be very much in the class pudding, won't it?

So please try some of the methods we've suggested here as you prepare yourself to teach and when you actually do teach. See what works for you and what doesn't. Not every technique "fits" everyone or every class, but we hope we've supplied a sufficient variety of skills and approaches for you to find something of use.

In exchange for anything we've been able to give you through this book, we'd like to ask one favor of you. Long after you've read these words, when you've been teaching for awhile, sometime, when you're sitting in the audience at a conference presentation or workshop or when you're a student in a class, just ask yourself this question:

Would I rather be up there performing than sitting back here?

When you honestly answer that question, "Yes," you'll have learned the real secret of teaching. Because what every real teacher knows is that it's much more fun to teach than to just sit and watch. You'll find yourself yearning to be part of the presentation every time. And from that point, there's no looking back. You've become a library teacher.

Index